Industrial Retardation in Britain
1880–1914

Industrial Retardation
in Britain
1880-1914

A. L. LEVINE

WEIDENFELD AND NICOLSON
5 Winsley Street London W1

To Fay

5, 57, 60, 62, 68, 70, 71, 72, 73, 7&.

Made and printed in Great Britain by
The Garden City Press Limited
Letchworth, Hertfordshire

113-5 116 118 119, 120, 121, 122, 123, 124

125-9   128

Contents

List of Tables

vii

Preface

This study springs from an old interest in the quality of the British industrial performance during the closing decades of the nineteenth century and the first decade and a half of the present century, a period which witnessed a marked quickening in the pace of technical and organizational change in the manufacturing industries of the major industrial powers. How did British manufacturing industry perform when there were now, indisputably, two other great industrial powers? (Others – academic economists, notably Marshall, parliamentarians, men of business, trade unionists – had asked the same question.)

The quality of Britain's performance could be viewed in terms of the 'goodness', 'badness' or 'up-to-dateness' of the *techniques* employed in British industry, using contemporary manufacturing practice in the United States and Germany as the norms. This is roughly what we have chosen to do. Granted the appropriateness of international comparisons, what are the *measures* of 'goodness' or 'badness' in this context? Here the economist usually reckons in terms of real costs or productivities, and it could be argued that these and other purely quantitative aspects of the performance story should form the centrepiece. However, the intriguing part of the story does not lie in the observed differences in real cost or productivity *per se*, but, rather, in those factors which may have led to differences in manufacturing methods (and hence in productivity). We therefore chose certain Anglo-American, and, to a lesser extent, Anglo-German, dissimilarities in manufacturing technique – evidenced, in part, by differences in labour productivity – as the *initial* substantive issues for an examination of Britain's manufacturing performance of six and seven decades ago, and the possible social and economic progenitors of these differences, in the case of Britain, as the *major* substantive issues.

The 'facts' of the alleged lag form an oft-told and not inordinately controversial story. This is not to suggest that the 'facts' are beyond dispute: some would contend that the term 'retardation' is an ill-chosen one in the present context. The possible reasons why – and here is where the real controversy lies – have also received attention, but not nearly the critical attention, and analysis, they deserve.

The author's personal debt to others is considerable. Thanks are owing, first of all, to Mr H. L. Beales who provided the initial stimulus from which the present study grew, and to Professor E. H. Phelps Brown who read the first draft of the manuscript and from whose critical comments the author benefited greatly. Thanks are also due to Mr M. D. Steuer, Professor S. B. Saul and Professor D. R. Pullman who read the entire manuscript and made many helpful suggestions. A great debt of gratitude is owing to Professor Basil Yamey who offered numerous comments and, above all, encouragement. Needless to add, responsibility for all errors of omission and commission rests with the author.

Finally, the author wishes to acknowledge his gratitude to the Nuffield Foundation whose generosity enabled him to complete the study.

PART 1

'*Sixty years ago England had . . . leadership in most branches of industry . . . It was inevitable that she should cede much of that leadership to the great land which attracts alert minds of all nations to sharpen their inventive and resourceful faculties by impact on one another. It was inevitable that she should yield a little of it to that land of great industrial traditions which yoked science in the service of man with unrivalled energy. It was not inevitable that she should lose so much of it as she has done.*'

ALFRED MARSHALL, *The Fiscal Policy of International Trade.*[1]

'*[England] shows traces of American enterprise and German order, but the enterprise is faded and the order muddled. They combine to a curious travesty in which activity and perseverance assume the expression of ease and indolence. The once enterprising manufacturer has grown slack, he has let the business take care of itself, while he is shooting grouse or yachting in the Mediterranean.*'

A. SHADWELL, *Industrial Efficiency. A Comparative Study of Industrial Life in England, Germany and America.*[2]

'*The American workers do not work any harder than their English brethren, the tendency being to use improved machinery of the latest type, and should a new machine be put in today and a better one come out tomorrow that will turn out more work it will be put on one side for the latest and best . . .*'

Report by W. C. Steadman, Parliamentary Committee of the TUC, in Mosely Industrial Commission to the United States of America, 1902, *Reports of the Delegates.*[3]

'. . . *it became a commonplace to contrast the antiquated industrial plant of England with the progressive, up-to-date character of the German industry.*'

R. J. S. HOFFMAN, *Great Britain and the German Trade Rivalry, 1875–1914.*[4]

[1] Parliamentary Papers, 1908, Vol. CVII (321), p 21.
[2] New ed. (London, Longmans, 1909), p 653.
[3] Manchester, 1903, p 258.
[4] Philadelphia, University of Pennsylvania Press, 1933, p 97.

3

'*In conclusion, I can only say that if we are to hold our own in the commerce of the world, both masters and men must be up and doing. Old methods must be dropped, old machinery abandoned. Practical education of the masses must be instituted and carried out upon a logical basis, and with efficiency.*'

A. MOSELY, in the preface to Mosely Industrial Commission to the USA, *op. cit.*[1]

[1] p 12.

1

Introduction

The Plan

It is intended, first of all, to attempt to validate the hypothesis that on the whole the British industries of six and more decades ago – the concern will be primarily with manufacturing industries – lagged behind the industries of the United States and Germany from the point of view of technology and organization (the implicit criterion of technological and organizational excellence here being that of productive effectiveness, or, simply, productivity). It is in this sense, and in this sense only, that the term retardation is here used.

The facts of the alleged retardation in British manufacturing industry are set out in Part 2. Instances of relative lag in the realm of technology (narrowly defined) are recorded in Chapter 2. A discussion of weakness with respect to the organization of production forms the subject matter of Chapter 3.

Secondly, and more importantly, it is intended to examine possible reasons for the condition of technical and organizational backwardness in British industry during the period in question. This examination forms the subject matter of Part 3. Chapter 4 deals with the question of the quality of British entrepreneurship and management as a possible retardative factor, with some of the social and social-psychological wellsprings of entrepreneurial-managerial behaviour and of working-class attitudes to technical change in industry, and with some of the more obvious educational constraints on the performance of entrepreneurs, managers, foremen and skilled workers in British industry. Chapter 5 examines the contentious question of trade union job-protective and income-protective policies as retardative factors. Chapter 6 is devoted to the possible economic causes of the alleged backwardness in British industry.

Some Features of Industrial Change in Britain, 1880–1914: Two Perspectives

Many years ago, a well-known historian of British socialism wrote that

> British industrial life [had] since 1880 been undergoing profound changes ... Indeed, since 1880 and in a more profound degree since 1900 a new factory system had arisen which [bore] the same relation to the factory system of the beginning of the nineteenth century as intensive cultivation to extensive agriculture, or, better still, as the modern armies to the old ones [1].

True, the changes in British industrial life had been profound. But most of the new industrial techniques had been developed rather more fully in countries other than Britain. It is possible, therefore, to have two quite different perspectives on the British industrial history of the closing decades of the nineteenth century and the first decade and a half of the present century. On the one hand, it is possible to speak of a second industrial revolution in Britain as elsewhere during these years. However, since the revolution proceeded rather more vigorously in the United States and Germany, one can also discern *relative* technical and organizational lag in Britain during the same period.

(a) A SECOND INDUSTRIAL REVOLUTION [2]

Among the more spectacular facets of this second industrial revolution was a continuing but unprecedented advance of the machine technique [3]. Machines were still being introduced for the first time into certain formerly wholly hand processes, and, in addition, various of the already existing machines and machine tools were either being replaced by more automatic prototypes or being transformed into instruments of greater automaticity of movement. Instances of the mechanization of hand processes are provided by boot and shoe manufacturing, some of the operations involved in the erection of the hull of a ship (thanks to the introduction of pneumatic and hydraulic power tools), and typesetting. The displacement of handwork by power-driven machinery in the boot and shoe trade is to be associated with the introduction of the factory system into that trade, which was among the last of the solely handcraft, homeworking, and small master industries to surrender to factory organization.

The development and spread of the automatic principle during the eighteen-eighties, 'nineties and early years of the present century was something rather more novel. Examples of the spread of automatism are to be found in the growing use of more automatic types of turret lathe, the appearance of the automatic screw machine, the Northrop automatic loom, and the Owens automatic glass bottle-making machine.

None of these would have been possible without major improvements in the accuracy of machining. Of the utmost importance, therefore, for the progress of mechanization and automatism was the advent during these years of what was virtually a new era of precision in machining. It was a new era made possible by improvements in the science of measurement, by the conversion of machine tools into instruments of greater precision, by a growing dependence around the end of the century upon one of the newer machine tools, the milling machine, and by the introduction of a practicable machine for fine grinding (a device which came into fairly widespread use only after the turn of the century).

No description of technological change during the second industrial revolution would be complete without mention of the new iron and steel technology. This rested principally upon the development of the basic process and the open hearth furnace and included – this was of supreme importance to the new mechanical engineering – the development of new high-speed tool steels. Finally (and it is to these, no doubt, that the popular imagination turns as soon as the words, 'second industrial revolution', are mentioned), the period saw a growing use of electricity as a source of motive power, and an increasing awareness of the role that chemistry should play in industry.

The story of the second industrial revolution does not end with technology, in the narrow sense. It was also a matter of environmental and organizational change. Thus, of tremendous importance was the continued evolution of the twin principles of division of labour or subdivision of process, and specialization of output. In some pursuits during these years subdivision of process had been carried to extreme lengths relative to what had been the case in the past. In engineering, for example, increasing division of labour had completely transformed what had at one time been the craft of the turner, and in the boot and shoe trade, division of labour (together with the spread of the machine technique) had revolutionized a whole series of productive operations. Specialization of output, or of plant, although not nearly as ubiquitous as the tendency to increasing subdivision of process within individual productive units, was also becoming rather more common both before and after the turn of the century.

If specialization of output on the part of individual plants becomes widespread enough, there exists an important precondition for the *standardization* of manufactured articles (or reducing the number of prototypes) on a broader basis than that provided by a single plant or firm. In Britain, although broadly based standardization of product was scarcely among the key trends then altering the face of industry, there was nevertheless evidence of some progress in this direction. One aspect of standardization, the standardization of component parts or interchangeability, was spreading a little more rapidly – at least on an intra-plant basis – than standardization of finished products. This was a consequence not only of rearrangements of productive operations, but of the new mechanical engineering.

Yet another prominent feature of organizational change during the period was the growth in the size of plants and of firms, the latter including both vertical and horizontal integration of individual productive units.

The most striking and, at the same time, most far-reaching, consequences of this continuing revolution in technology and organization were the increase in the tempo of production and widespread increases in productivity. These were the result not only of increasing mechanization, automatism, division of labour, standardization, and growth in the size of plant and firm, but, also, of increases in the operating speeds of machinery and, equally important, of resort to various managerial devices for increasing the productivity of labour. Greatly enhanced operating speeds for metal cutting were made possible by the appearance, very shortly after 1900, of a new and extremely high-speed steel for cutting tools. The newer devices for managing and directing the labour force arose out of greater concentration by management upon the effectiveness of the labour factor's performance and upon problems of labour supervision in general. As a result, various schemes were devised for extracting from labour greater attentiveness and increased effort. Such schemes usually involved both closer supervision of the worker's actual performance on the job and the provision of wage incentives. As to the former, there was a noticeable tightening up of shop discipline in the matter of time-keeping. Mechanical time recorders first began to be used extensively during this period. In many engineering establishments, an attempt was made to increase labour productivity by the use of 'feed and speed' supervisors. However, if stricter supervision was being increasingly relied upon to maximize effort, so too were incentives. Thus, new systems of payment by results rather more sophisticated than simple piece-work were being developed. The outstanding example of such schemes was the premium bonus plan, bitterly opposed by the trade union movement. But inducement had its gentler side as well, for these were the halcyon years of profit-sharing, co-partnership, and similar plans for worker participation in earnings and decision-making. Such devices also met with marked hostility from the unions. In any event, these schemes were not markedly successful.

Some of the technical and organizational changes in manufacturing industry during these years were linked with the appearance, or more rapid growth, of certain entirely new trades. Such for example were the sewing machine, cycle, electrical, and motor vehicle trades. The sewing machine trade underwent considerable development during this period. (Its early history actually pre-dates the period, since it first came into prominence during the eighteen-sixties and eighteen-seventies.) The cycle trade enjoyed its first major expansion during the last decade and a half of the nineteenth century, when the new mechanical engineering was becoming a part of the natural order of things. The principal growth of the electrical trades was a slightly later development, while the rise of the motor vehicle industry was almost entirely a post-1900 phenomenon. The beginnings and subsequent expansion of these industries is in part to be attributed to the newer methods of machining, to subdivision of process, and to the practice of the interchangeable system. On the other hand, it could be said that the expansion of these industries was itself a constant spur to the development of new methods of production and new machines. For example, the spread and further development of the interchangeable system were promoted by the growth of these industries, the cycle trade being of special significance here. Then, too, both the cycle trade and the motor trade stimulated the invention and perfection of certain new machines and machine tools. A notable example is provided by the gearcutting machine [4]. Finally, and of the utmost importance, is the fact that in the manufacture of things like sewing machines and bicycles, there were discernible, even prior to the turn of the century, elements of what a later generation came to call the 'mass production technique'; a technique embodying to an exceptional degree the automatic principle, division of labour and standardization, and characterized above all by swiftness and continuity, and by operations conducted on a massive scale.

(b) RETARDATION

The development of the mass production technique was not a British contribution to industrial progress. Nor were most of the other innovations that constituted the technical and organizational progress in manufacturing industry sixty and seventy years ago. In mechanical engineering, founding, typesetting, bottle-making, and weaving, the United States can lay claim to most of the important mechanical inventions of the period; while in metallurgy, both France and Germany can claim important technical advances over what were, in some cases, originally British contributions. Two new machine tools, the universal miller and the grinding machine, which had helped make the new mechanical engineering a reality, were American inventions. So, too, was the Linotype machine which displaced handwork in typesetting, and the Tabor moulding machine which displaced handwork in foundries. The evolution of the turret lathe along more automatic lines and the invention of the automatic screw-making lathe were other American contributions to the development of the machine technique and the automatic principle. And the American achievement in the realm of automatic machines also included the Northrop automatic loom (invented by a British emigrant to the United States) and the Owens automatic glass bottle-making machine. In iron and steel making, French and German contributions loom large and include, in the case of France, an important addition to Siemens's original contribution to the development of the open-hearth furnace, and, in the case of Germany, some major steps forward in electrical metallurgy (although here, too, Sir William Siemens's pioneering efforts must be recognized). The British achievement of these years does, however, include three inventions of the utmost importance—the first application of Siemens's regenerative furnace to steel-making (that is, the above-mentioned open-hearth process), the Thomas and Gilchrist basic steel-making process, and the Parsons steam turbine.

Whatever their national origin, all of these new devices and processes were sooner or later introduced into British industry. But, except for the open-hearth process, there was a decided difference between Britain and the other two great industrial powers as regards the rate of adoption and diffusion. By and large, British industry did not innovate as rapidly as the industries of the other countries. In some areas of British industry, there appeared to be almost a deification of a technological *status quo*. Perhaps the most piquant case of failure to adopt new methods is provided by the Thomas-Gilchrist basic steel process. This enormously important new process was a British invention, but Britain lagged terribly behind Germany and the United States when it came to changing over from the older acid to the new basic process. It was the same story with a host of other new devices and techniques. (As Charles Wilson has written,) 'What was really serious was not so much that fewer inventions were being generated but that fewer were being incorporated into industrial practice.' [5]

Then, too, the world's foremost industrial power of yesteryear had suffered itself to fall behind not only with respect to making use of new inventions, but with respect to adopting new methods of organizing productive operations. This was particularly true of those methods that collectively comprise the mass production technique – specialization, standardization, continuity of operation, and massive scale. Over half a century ago, a student of British industry wrote of certain of the great Sheffield steel mills that 'some of the departments . . . are quite out of date, not so much in equipment as in construction and organization' [6]. (He took care, however, to exonerate the newer Sheffield steel works, which he considered 'quite admirable in every respect' [7].) Certainly, notorious examples of out-of-date organization and inadequate scale of operation could be found elsewhere in British industry.

The fact that some of the newer industries – the motor trade, the electrical industry, and the chemical industry, to cite three especially prominent examples – did not grow as rapidly in Britain as they did in the United States and Germany (Germany should be left out of the motor trade comparison) is to be accounted yet another instance of industrial-technical lag in Britain.

It is often thought that critics who questioned the technical and organizational condition of the Workshop of the World first made themselves heard during the 'eighties, 'nineties and early years of the present century. The truth is that observations concerning technical and other lags in British industry, and using American practice as a point of reference, were being made at least as early as the eighteen-fifties. In 1853 and 1854 two British commissions visited industrial areas in the United States. One of them reported on the New York Industrial Exhibition and included among its members Joseph Whitworth [8]. The other was sponsored by the Ordnance Department and reported on industrial machinery in the United States [9]. Both commissions rang the praises of American industry, pointing, among other things, to the extent of mechanization in American industry, the use of specialized machines and machine tools, the degree of standardization of manufactured wares, the volume of output, and the methods of organizing and arranging productive operations.

Later on, Anglo-American comparisons, usually adverse to British industry, were to become a commonplace. Indeed, during the eighteen-nineties and first decade of the twentieth century, there was quite widespread agreement with the British trade unionist who, just returned from the United States, had written, 'There is no doubt that the leading mills of American manufacture are far ahead of our own best mills in their arrangement and outputs. I have seen nothing like it in this country – either in the matter of output or labour-saving appliances.' [10] He had been on a trade union delegation which visited the United States in 1902, which was sponsored by a British business man, and which was one of the forerunners of many later pilgrimages and commissions of inquiry. He spoke of the steel industry, but similar opinions came from several of his colleagues who represented other trades. At any rate, fifteen of his colleagues had replied in the affirmative to the question, 'Do you consider American factories better equipped for production than English?' [11] (Three had returned negative answers, and three were equivocal in their replies.) And unfavourable opinions of Britain's industrial performance were not confined to trade unionists. In fact, there was a growing body of individuals who, during the 'eighties, 'nineties, and early years of the present century, felt that Britain was slipping badly as a great industrial power, or at least as a great industrial power that was highly receptive to innovation.

There was of course no unanimity on the question, for there were those who were ready to deny any suggestion that British industry and British industrialists were not abreast of the best that could be found elsewhere. The denials were most vociferous in the iron and steel trades. (Interestingly enough, these were the trades which seemed at times to be bearing the brunt of the criticism.) One wonders whether, on occasion, a propensity to shrug off criticism did not spring from national pride. This is always a problem in the evaluation of those international comparisons that are made by 'committed' observers. Certainly, many of those nineteenth-century industrialists who had contributed to and then observed with pride Britain's industrial supremacy were, understandably, prone to defend and extol, even when the ground being defended had eroded somewhat. Was it lingering pride in Britain's past achievement rather than acute awareness of the present which prompted Sir Lowthian Bell, a great iron and steel magnate of the period, to write that 'I have seen no smelting works in the old world or new which could compare with the Middlesbrough practice'? [12] On the other hand, a concession was occasionally made to the critics. It 'is probably not too much to claim that British practice is equal to anything in the world,' wrote the secretary of the British Iron Trade Association in 1902, 'excepting, perhaps, two or three of the most forward establishments on the other side of the Atlantic.' [13] The emphasis here is still on the excellence of British practice. Other observers would admit that all had not been too well in the past, only to insist that the short-comings had been eliminated, and that from the point of view of technique British industry had nothing to be ashamed of in the present (the present usually being the five or ten years prior to the First World War) [14]. On at least one occasion *The Economist* took this line with regard to the iron and steel trade (although notice that *The Economist* had its reservations, too).

We have heard much from time to time of our antiquated appliances and out-of-date methods, but within the past year or two a marked change for the better has been effected in our iron and steel industries ... a change which has not been much advertised, as is the case with some of our rivals' improvements, but a change which no one closely acquainted with these trades can fail to recognize. Improved types of furnaces and machinery have been adopted by all our principal firms recently, the latest and best appliances invented at home and abroad are now being employed, more practical and better trained men are at the head of departments, vast economies, both in labour and materials, are being effected and, in the words of Sir Charles M'Laren, 'it is not too much to say that the steel plants now in Cleveland, in Lanarkshire, in South Wales, and the Midlands, are well ahead of anything that can be found abroad'.

It is true that in the past we were not always as alert as we might have been, and that we allowed rivals to get ahead of us in some cases; it may be true today that we do not display an ever-ready adaptability to new ideas, times, and circumstances; . . . but, for all that, there need not be much anxiety concerning our future as an iron-producing and manufacturing country. [15]

This was written early in 1906. Some months later, a similar note was struck.

The problem of trade is, primarily, the problem of cheap and efficient production, and much has been done in the last four or five years to cheapen production in our steel trade. In the first place, it is not too much to say that, so far as labour costs are concerned, an entirely new policy has recently been adopted. More practical and alert managers and foremen – 'six o'clock' managers – are now controlling our works and workers. The old methods of slackness and of social and family influences, which have hitherto cursed British industry, have well nigh been abolished. There has recently been a speeding-up, all round. Secondly, vastly improved appliances have been adopted. The reproach about old-fashioned machinery and out-of-date furnaces in Britain scarcely holds good any longer. The best inventions are now to be found in British as well as in American and German workshops. [16]

The author of the first quotation did, however, admit that 'it may be true today that we do not display an ever-ready adaptability to new ideas, times, and circumstances; . . .' That, surely, was the nub of the matter. Slowness to adapt, slowness to receive new ideas and install new processes – these were the charges that struck home.

If Britain began to lag behind the United States and Germany as regards the adoption of new industrial techniques, it would be expected that the *rate of growth* of productivity [17] in British industry would begin to lag behind productivity growth rates in the industries of the other two countries and that eventually there might appear marked differences in absolute levels of productivity. There is statistical evidence available showing that in individual sectors, and in aggregate, British industry did in fact fall behind in regard to the rate of increase of productivity, and, eventually, in absolute levels of productivity as well. According to Professor Frankel's estimates (Table 1), the average annual rates of growth of the physical productivity of labour in manufacturing industry as a whole, in Britain and America, were of approximately the same order of magnitude for the period 1870–90, with Britain possibly retaining a tiny lead.

14

However, during the period 1890–1907, the average annual rate of increase in American productivity was, according to the same estimates, twenty times the British rate of increase. For the entire period, 1870–1907, the American average annual rate of increase appears to have been about two-and-a-third times the British. Data for Germany, for the same period, are rather less reliable. However, it is possible that for the period between 1873–83 and 1908–13, the *trend* rate of growth of productivity in German manufacturing industry was as high as 2·6 per cent per annum, which compares with an American trend rate of 1·6 per cent for the same period [18], and (to make use of Professor Frankel's data which are not strictly comparable, since they refer to average annual instead of trend rates) with a British average annual rate of well under one per cent for a roughly comparable period (1870–1907).

TABLE 1

Average Annual Percentage Increases in Labour Productivity in British and American Manufacturing Industry, 1870–1937

Period	Annual percentage increase in physical output per worker	
	United Kingdom	United States
	%	%
1870–1907	0·6	1·4
1870–1890	1·0	0·9
1890–1907	0·1	2·0
1907–1937	1·4	1·8
1907–1924	0·5	1·8
1924–1937	2·4	1·8

SOURCE: M. Frankel, *British and American Manufacturing Productivity*, *A Comparison and Interpretation* (Urbana, Ill., Bureau of Economic and Business Research, University of Illinois, 1957), p 103.

The different rates of growth of productivity eventually yielded marked differences in the absolute levels of productivity. Using estimates for 1907/1909 prepared by Taussig, the American–British ratios of physical productivity for a group of six industries were as follows: pig iron, 2·2; steel, 3·1; tinplate, 3·9; cement, 2·0; sugar refining, 1·7 to 2·1; flour milling, 1·5 [19]. (Note that in each case the product is a fairly homogeneous one, which eliminates some of the difficulties inherent in productivity comparisons.) These results should be compared with the net value productivity ratios prepared by A. W. Flux for thirteen industrial groups in Britain and the United States for the same years. (See Table 2.) Again, the American productivity advantage is shown to be considerable.

TABLE 2

Ratios of Net Value of Output per Person Employed, United States and United Kingdom, Selected Industries, 1907/1909

Industrial Group	Net Value of output per person employed, American–British ratios, 1907/1909[a]
Textiles	2·00
Clothing	2·76
Leather	2·44
Paper and printing	2·44
Lumber and timber	1·79
Pottery, glass, and building materials	2·28
Chemicals, dyes, drugs, oils, etc.	2·00
Iron and steel	2·37
Engineering and shipbuilding	2·17
Vehicles	2·16
Non-ferrous metals	2·59
Miscellaneous	2·31
Food and tobacco	2·28
All Groups	2·26

[a] The American data are for 1909, the British for 1907.

SOURCE: A. W. Flux, 'Industrial Productivity in Great Britain and the United States', *Quarterly Journal of Economics*, Vol. 48, November 1933, p 27.

When did this disparity in productivities first become apparent? Referring again to *rates of increase*, it will be noticed (Table 1) that the American–British difference in the aggregate rate of growth of productivity in manufacturing industry was being widened during the period under consideration, especially during the years 1890–1907. If Frankel's data for the average annual percentage increase are extrapolated backwards, the result is approximate equality in the aggregate productivity ratio for the two countries in 1830 [20]. Frankel treats the results of his extrapolations with caution, and merely states that the available evidence lends 'credence to the hypothesis that American productivity began to forge ahead of British productivity somewhere between 1830 and 1860' [21].

Regardless of when Anglo-American productivity differences first became apparent, the existence of marked productivity differences between British and American manufacturing industries during the last decade of the nineteenth century, and later years, is beyond dispute. There is little doubt that productivity was *growing* more rapidly in German industry, too, than in British industry during the period under consideration. At any rate, productivities in German industries – especially in the coal and metallurgical complex – were already higher than in these same industries in Britain, late in the nineteenth century.

Britain's slower rate of productivity growth may surely be taken as evidence of some degree of technical and organizational lag in British industry. In fact, it appears that the Anglo-American (and Anglo-German) productivity differentials sprang *primarily* from the relative backwardness of British industrial technique [22].

True, the productivity differences might have sprung from other sources as well. First of all, there is the question of Britain's natural resource disadvantages: what did these contribute to the observed productivity differences? The quality and variety of a nation's natural resource endowment can impinge upon the productivity of its industries in two ways. First, the resource base can influence productivity directly through its effect upon real labour costs: that is, an inferior resource base can result in a higher input of fabricating activity or labour (as well as materials) relative to output. Secondly, the resource base can influence (labour) productivity indirectly through its effect upon choice of techniques. Here we shall confine ourselves to the direct effects upon real labour costs. (The influence of the resource base upon choice of techniques will be examined in Chapter 6.)

Especially significant was Britain's relatively inferior endowment of metallic resources – an inferiority which was not entirely offset by Britain's commanding position as a world trader. The production of pig iron is an example. A few years before the war, it required on the average 2·48 tons of ore and cinder (limestone) to produce a ton of pig iron in Britain, as against 1·96 tons in the United States. [23].

17

Importation of foreign ore in the British case did not eliminate this real cost difference which was undoubtedly one of the factors behind the observed difference in labour productivity in the production of pig iron in the two countries. On the other hand, in many of the capital-intensive industries, especially those in which mechanized fabricating activity was a major component of the total input, far outweighing the importance of the materials input, the quality of the materials consumed could not be considered as being of decisive importance as regards labour productivity. A fortiori, this would apply to the fuels consumed in many of the capital-intensive, highly mechanized industrial processes.

No doubt it is better to be bounteously endowed with natural resources than to be without such an endowment. After all, ample and rich domestic sources of raw materials reduce exposure to the uncertainties of dependence upon external supplies of raw materials, and help develop new skills and bring viability, flexibility, and adaptability into the body economic. [24]. Still, when the real cost argument is seen in its proper perspective, and when the part that international trade played in reducing the resource imbalance is given its due, it can scarcely be maintained that the relative inferiority of the British resource base was *the* causal factor behind the lagging rate of growth of productivity in Britain's industries. True, the resource argument is not wholly irrelevant in the case of certain primary-processing industries. But Professor Frankel's cross-sectional study of American–British productivity differences lends very little support to a resource argument which is offered as *the* explanation of the lower productivities in a wide variety of British industries. As Frankel has demonstrated, the productivity differentials were not confined to industries in which resource considerations might be deemed to have been important: the higher productivities of American industry cut across such lines. Possibly the most telling argument against the resource explanation of productivity differences lies in the fact that during the last decade of the nineteenth century, the productivity gap between Britain and the United States was widening much more rapidly than was the resource gap. In fact, rates of mineral resource depletion in the United States during this period might even have produced some *narrowing* of the resource gap. And it was this period which witnessed a great surge forward in industrial technique in all advanced countries, but much more so in the United States (and Germany) than in Britain.

Other students of the problem might be inclined to regard differences in capital intensity as *the* explanation of the observed productivity differences. No indisputably accurate data for an Anglo-American comparison of capital intensity are available for the period under consideration, but Rostas's ratios of mechanical horsepower per worker in factory trades for selected years from 1899 to 1925 [25], and employment and horsepower data for thirteen industrial groups for the years 1924/1925 published by Flux [26], indicate, not surprisingly, markedly greater capital intensity in American manufacturing industry than in British. No doubt comparable differentials obtained for the period 1880–99. The question is whether or not higher American capital–labour ratios are to be looked upon as the principal cause of the productivity differences. While the available data do not permit a categorical denial of this possibility, neither do they afford unqualified support. Professor Frankel has correlated first the American–British ratios of fuel input per worker (this being the indicator of capital intensity chosen) for twenty-six industries for the years 1947/1948, and second, the American–British ratios of output per worker for these same industries. The resulting coefficient of correlation was only 0·43 [27]. Flux's data for 1924/1925 show that the American–British capital intensity differentials (capital intensity in this instance was measured by mechanical horsepower per employee) may even have been *negatively* correlated with the productivity differentials. (See Table 3. The rank correlation coefficient is —0·61.) Finally, Flux's data, and the horsepower per employee ratios computed from them, should be compared to Rostas's data for the interwar period on labour productivity and horsepower per worker in twenty-eight British and American industries – data which do not 'suggest any close correlation between the relative amount of horsepower per worker and relative productivity' [28].

It should, however, be pointed out that the measure of capital intensity adopted by Professor Frankel (fuel input per worker) and the measures made use of in the earlier studies of Flux and Rostas (mechanical horsepower per worker) are rather more symptomatic of differences in *mechanization* than of capital intensity *per se*. Viewed in this light, the findings of Frankel, Flux, and Rostas merely indicate that American manufacturing industry was rather more mechanized than British – a not very startling conclusion – and that the productivity of American labour was higher than the productivity of British labour. The differences in degree of mechanization form part of the larger story of technical and organizational lag in British industry. It was not only a question of the sheer volume of mechanization per employee, but it was also a question of the kinds of machines in use, of the up-to-dateness of these machines, and of the excellence of the organization of the plant and productive processes

TABLE 3

Output and Horsepower per Employee, American–British Ratios, 1924/1925[a]

Industrial Group	Net output per employee, American–British ratio	Mechanical horsepower per employee, American–British ratio
Engineering and shipbuilding	3·34	1·36
Iron and steel	3·21	1·45
Clothing	3·19	1·75
Chemicals, dyes, drugs, oils, etc.	3·04	1·58
Non-ferrous metals	2·97	1·93
Vehicles	2·91	1·84
Pottery, glass, and building materials	2·91	2·85
Miscellaneous	2·88	1·78
Leather	2·56	1·80
Paper and printing	2·55	3·04
Food and tobacco	2·36	4·62
Lumber and timber	2·28	2·21
Textiles	2·28	1·45

[a] The British data are for 1924, the American for 1925.

SOURCES: Col. (1), Flux, *op. cit.*, p 7, Table B.

Col. (2), computed from Flux, *op. cit.*, p 6, Table A.

that made use of these machines. Therefore, simple correlation between international differences in fuel input per worker (or any similar measure of mechanization) and international differences in labour productivity cannot provide complete enough corroboration for assumptions concerning mechanization and labour productivity. *A fortiori*, this applies to preconceptions concerning capital intensity and labour productivity [29].

International differences in productivity may also derive, in part, from international differences in the structure of demand. Precisely how important were demand or market considerations in inducing the observed productivity differentials? Quantitative precision is of course not possible here. Rostas's study of the data for the interwar years led him to conclude that 'After allowance has been made for [demand] factors, [Anglo-American] differences in relative productivity would perhaps become smaller, but they would still exist in practically all of the industries that have been analysed' [30]. (Admittedly, as will be seen in Chapter 6, the structure of demand can affect the choice of technique and hence influence productivity indirectly.)

Finally, it is conceivable that the Anglo-American productivity differentials sprang to some extent from qualitative and other differences in the labour forces of the two countries. Thus it could be argued that because of social, cultural, physical, or other factors, the average level of personal efficiency, or the quality and quantity of the input of effort of British workers was inferior to that of American workers. Lack of evidence makes it well-nigh impossible to pronounce on the matter [31]. (The less direct influence of working-class attitudes to innovation and possible trade union barriers to the flow of new techniques will be considered in Chapters 4 and 5.)

In sum, therefore, we would suggest that the slower rate of growth of productivity in British industry as compared to American industry (or to German industry), and the generally lower productivities in individual British industries at any point of time during the period 1880–1914, were functions, primarily, of weaknesses or lag in technology and organization in British industry rather than of an inferior endowment of natural resources, differences in capital intensity, differences in the structure of demand, or differences in the quality of the labour inputs of the two countries. The productivity differences are thus to be regarded as evidence of the lag in technique.

It can of course be argued that although differences in labour productivity may be indicative of differences in effectiveness of industrial technique, labour productivity alone does not provide a broad enough test of industrial efficiency considered as a totality, or as an aggregate input–output relationship. That is, since labour is practically never the sole factor of production employed in any productive process – typically, labour is combined with fuel, raw materials, capital facilities and other inputs – the production functions of all inputs must be taken into account if one is to obtain an accurate picture of the efficiency of any given productive activity.

Or, to put the same argument in slightly different terms, if labour productivity is used as an index of industrial efficiency, the measure of labour productivity usually adopted – that is, the ratio of output to the input of the labour *directly* involved – can never be an accurate indicator of efficiency and will in fact frequently be grossly misleading. The only meaningful ratio, if it is desired to measure industrial efficiency on the basis of labour as the lowest common denominator input, is one which takes into account not only the labour directly involved, but, also, all the labour 'embodied' in the capital goods and other material inputs, or the labour *indirectly* involved in the productive operation as well. Only if such a measure is devised can labour productivity ever be made to serve as an indicator of industrial efficiency [32]. However, while it is true that on the level of the individual firm labour productivity (narrowly defined) will rarely be the best indicator of all-round efficiency, when, on the other hand, one makes productivity comparisons between two national economies and differences in labour productivity (again narrowly defined) are found to exist in the case of practically every industry, as in the Anglo-American comparison, there is an extremely strong *prima facie* case for the existence of differences in *aggregate* real cost (or 'efficiency') – that is, taking into account *all* factors of production – in the two economies being compared [33]. This becomes obvious as soon as it is realized that advanced economies are in essence concatenations of industrial complexes wherein the outputs of a wide variety of industries serve as inputs for other industries.

Admittedly, this may still not satisfy the critics, for it is conceivable, or at least arithmetically possible, that while the productivity of labour may be uniformly lower in the industries of one country as compared to these same industries in another country, the productivity of *capital* may be uniformly higher (possibly because of the *type* of capital equipment in use) and thus provide an offset, or partial offset, to the higher real costs of labour. But this is rather unlikely, especially if the differences in labour productivities are of a considerable order of magnitude. In any event, it would appear that Britain's lower labour productivities were not counter-balanced by markedly higher productivities of capital. Difficulties of measurement here are of course immense, but the available evidence, for all its shortcomings, is adequate enough to reveal the presence of great disparities in capital productivity in the two countries, if there were such disparities. In Table 4, the gross value of output [34] is shown for

22

TABLE 4

Gross Value of Output per Horsepower of Engines and Motors Installed in Manufacturing Industry, United Kingdom and United States, 1905/1907[a]

Industrial Group	United Kingdom			United States		
	Gross Value of production ($'000)	Horse-power[b] ('000)	GVP per horse-power ($)	Gross Value of production ($'000)	Horse-power ('000)	GVP per horse-power ($)
Iron and steel, engineering, and shipbuilding	1,819,701	2,902	627	2,903,433	4,341	669
Metal trades other than iron and steel	453,305	104	4,359	922,262	344	2,681
Lumber and its remanufactures	224,992	188	1,197	1,223,730	2,250	544
Textile and clothing trades	2,161,488	2,197	984	2,147,441	1,862	1,153
Food trades	817,870	318	2,572	2,845,235	1,477	1,926
Drink and beverage trades	460,474	102	4,514	501,267	370	1,355
Tobacco trades	115,760	7	16,537	331,118	29	11,418
Chemical and allied trades	363,905	254	1,432	1,031,965	723	1,427
Leather trades	116,371	28	4,156	705,747	219	3,222
Clay, glass, and stone products	136,275	282	483	391,230	831	471
Paper, printing, and allied trades	297,344	274	1,085	857,117	1,357	632

[a] The UK data are for 1907, the US for 1905.

[b] Exclusive of rented power.

SOURCES: United Kingdom: Adapted from UK, *Final Report of the First Census of Production* [Cd. 6320] 1912, pp 18, 21, 478, 480, 482, 485, 490, 668, 671, 675.

United States: US Bureau of the Census, *Census of Manufactures, 1905*, Part I, *United States by Industries* (Washington, Government Printing Office, 1907), Table LXIII, p cxv, and Table 3, pp 26 *et seq*.

23

eleven industrial groups in the two countries in the years 1905 (United States) and 1907 (United Kingdom). While the industrial grouping leaves much to be desired, and the measure of output used may to some extent blur the differences in *physical* output, Table 4 nevertheless provides sufficient evidence to question the belief that the Anglo-American productivity differences were offset by considerably higher productivities of capital in Britain's industries. In fact, just the opposite appeared to be the case in the important iron and steel, engineering and shipbuilding group, and in the textile and clothing group. (Again, allowances must be made for the level of aggregation, especially in the case of the iron, steel, and cognate trades.) In the chemical trades, and in the clay, glass, and stone group, the output per horsepower ratios was exceedingly close in both countries. In only two cases – lumber and its remanufactures, and the drink and beverage trades – was the British ratio more than twice as high as the American. In other words, a powerful offsetting effect to the very considerable Anglo-American labour productivity differentials [35] in the shape of markedly lower real capital costs in Britain simply does not seem to have existed. Moreover, it should be borne in mind that the indicator of installed capital made use of in Table 4 is confined to sources of motive power and hence omits other types of mechanical equipment and, also, buildings and structures. If buildings and structures were included, the result could conceivably be a lowering of the British capital productivity ratios and an elevating of the American ratios. There are two possible reasons for this: first, a greater British propensity to build for 'the ages' as compared to contemporary American industrial building methods; and secondly, the possible presence of significant economies of scale as regards buildings, or the influence upon the (total) capital productivity ratio that a proliferation of smaller plants (United Kingdom) might have had as compared to the existence of a relatively smaller number of large plants (United States). Also, it should be observed that the measure of installed horsepower in the United Kingdom excludes rented horsepower. Inclusion of the latter would of course have lowered the British output per horsepower ratios [36]. Finally, the data in Table 4 might be compared to Flux's findings for 1924/1925. Out of the thirteen industrial groups considered by Flux, only four (paper and printing; lumber and timber; pottery, glass and building materials; and food and tobacco) showed a higher British ratio of net output per mechanical horsepower [37].

24

Admittedly, the 'efficiency' of the economist and the literature of economics is a notoriously static concept – a concept which usually has to do with output-maximizing or cost-minimizing deployments of resources, *given the techniques of production or the total (technical and organizational) milieu of production*. But the productive effectiveness or 'efficiency' which is of concern here, and which will be examined in some detail in Part 2, explicitly includes the possibility of varying the techniques of production and altering the industrial milieu. Our international comparisons of efficiency are placed within this kind of dynamic context, and are, in essence, comparisons of techniques and methods, and industrial performances, in which productivity – another essentially dynamic concept, since unlike the 'efficiency' of static economic analysis productivity has no upper limit, given the possibility of varying techniques and methods [38] – is made to serve as a rough measure of the effectiveness of the techniques or industrial performances being compared. Therefore, a great many of those rather defensive accounts of the British industrial achievement which concluded that British techniques were 'efficient', given the total environment of British industry, simply will not do, or, at least, are irrelevant to comparisons of industrial performance which are set within the context of *changing* techniques.

A Note on Sources

The shortcomings to be considered derive, ultimately, from comparison with American techniques and, to some extent, with German practice as well. But *whose* comparisons are to be relied upon? What constitutes reliable evidence in this sphere? Some observers were simply special pleaders who had a vested interest in a particular industrial or commercial *status quo*. Others, perfervent patriots, stubbornly defended their country's industries, no matter how cogent the reasoning of critics. Fortunately, there were also those who were rather more objective.

Valuable insights into the problems of industrial technique of six and seven decades ago are to be found scattered through the reports and minutes of evidence of royal commissions, government reports, the contemporary technical press and a variety of technical papers read to professional bodies, trade union documents, and, finally, a vast miscellany of the published opinions of persons technically well-informed and professionally well-qualified. Here, then, is where the story of backwardness in the British industry of the period is buried. Of particular value as sources of qualitative evidence are the Report and Minutes of Evidence of the Royal Commission on the Depression of Trade and Industry (1884–6), the Minutes of Evidence of the Royal Commission on Labour (1892–3), the Minutes of Evidence of the Royal Commission on the Poor Laws and Relief of Distress (1910), the reports of the departmental committees appointed by the Board of Trade during the First World War to consider the state of various British industries, and the surveys of the (Balfour) Committee on Industry and Trade which were published between 1927 and 1929. Additional information on British industrial practice may be garnered from the annual reports of the Chief Inspector of Factories and Workshops – actually, these are a veritable mine of information for the student of change in industrial technique – and from the voluminous *History of the Ministry of Munitions*. The reports of Joseph Chamberlain's 'Tariff Commission' (1907–9) stand in a class by themselves. The queries were tendentious, as were many of the replies. Still, if sharply critical judgment is brought to bear on these documents, they can be made to yield a great deal of evidence on the question of Britain's industrial performance [39].

The most reliable kind of technical data, and a host of accurate observations on industrial organization, may be found in *The Engineer* and in papers delivered to professional bodies such as the Institution of Mechanical Engineers [40]. Since standardization must play a critical role in any advanced industrial society, the annual reports (1905–14) of the old Engineering Standards Committee are of some importance. The same applies to some of the publications of those trade unions and trade unionists who were active in industries that may be considered 'sensitive' from the point of view of technological change. Especially valuable are the *Monthly Journal* and *Monthly Record and Report* of the Amalgamated Society of Engineers for the years 1900–14. Less useful, but of some value, are W. Mosses's *A History of the United Pattern Makers' Association, 1872–1922* and D. C. Cummings's *A Historical Survey of the Boiler Makers' and Iron and Steel Ship Builders' Society from August 1834 to August 1904*.

'Contemporary observer' covers a multitude of sins and sinners, but it includes at least a few individuals who could claim to both expertise and objectivity. Such a one was Arthur Shadwell, sometime industrial correspondent of *The Times*. His classic *Industrial Efficiency* (1909 edition) is both a wide-ranging critique and a comparison of

British industry to that of Germany and the United States. It is a model of fairness and apt observation. Other contemporary opinions that deserve attention may be found among the reports of the members of the Mosely Commission, a group of trade unionists assembled by a British entrepreneur who wished to expose the leaders of British labour to American industrial practice. Mosely sent his group – they were all high-ranking union officials and represented the country's major industries – to the United States in 1902. Their reports, which were published the following year, contain an enormous amount of data relevant to any discussion of comparative industrial efficiency.

PART 2

The Shortcomings

2

Technology

It is possible to single out at least four areas of weakness in the British industrial technology of sixty years ago. First, there was the matter of mechanization. Admittedly, there are in this realm no absolute canons of perfection. However, if we permit contemporary American practice to indicate the potential, then we must conclude that there was a considerable lag with respect to mechanization in a number of British industries. This is also true of the automatic principle, or, more precisely, of those examples, then few in number but each of tremendous significance, of the 'fully automatic' device. Secondly, there was what many considered a characteristically British pace of production. This provoked all manner of comment. Thirdly, there was the relative neglect of electrification. And, no amount of understanding, no explaining away of deleterious consequences, could acquit British manufacturers of electrical equipment of the charge of ineptitude and indifference, and, to press the point, of organizational chaos. Strong words, but the weakness in question provoked near-vituperation even from those who were not normally inclined to disparage the way things were done in British industry. Finally, there was the state of Britain's iron and steel technology. Some of the emphasis of the critics was doubtless misplaced, but much of it was embarrassingly apt.

Mechanization and the Automatic Principle

Mechanization means the installation and use of power-driven machinery. A possible measure, therefore, of the extent of mechanization in industry is the amount of horsepower available or in use per industrial worker [1]. The differences in the aggregate horsepower/worker ratios in British and American manufacturing industry [2] are too striking to be ignored. (See Table 5)

Of all the indictments brought against British industry and British

31

industrialists by contemporary observers at the turn of the century and later, the one most assiduously pressed was that of failure to mechanize, or, where mechanization was already the rule, of failure to make existing machines more automatic. Certainly, in the long list of Anglo-American comparisons provided by the members of the Mosely Commission there are repeated references to this shortcoming. 'There is much more extensive use of machinery in the

TABLE 5

Horsepower[a] Available per Operative in Factory Trades, United Kingdom and United States, 1899–1925

Year	Horsepower per Operative	
	United Kingdom	United States
1899	—	2·18
1907	1·37[b]	—
1909	—	2·88
1924	2·38	—
1925	—	4·37

[a] Horsepower of prime movers plus that of electric motors driven by purchased electricity.

[b] Approximate estimate.

SOURCE: L. Rostas, *Comparative Productivity in British and American Industry* (National Institute of Economic and Social Research, *Occasional Papers*, XIII; Cambridge, Cambridge University Press, 1948), p 68.

States than in Sheffield for cutlery purposes': thus Mr Holmshaw of the Sheffield Cutlery Council [3]. The representative of the Midland Counties Trades Federation observed that in tube manufacture in the United States 'machinery plays a more important part in the manufacture than in this country' [4]. This was also the opinion of G. N. Barnes of the Amalgamated Society of Engineers [5] and the delegate from the Amalgamated Society of Tailors [6]. The accuracy of these observations cannot be controverted. That the Sheffield cutlery trade stood behind its rivals in other countries as regards mechanization was a matter of frequent comment. No one could deny that the stamping of blades by machines, instead of forging them by hand, was being practised far more widely in Germany than in Britain at this time. The observation concerning the clothing

trades is borne out by ample corroborating evidence. Thus in the
Factory Report for 1914 we read that the 'slow development . . . of
the use of the power sewing machine in its manifold possibilities was
one of the biggest difficulties that had to be faced' on the outbreak
of war in August, 1914 [7].

Examples of backwardness with respect to mechanization also
included some of the great industries of the land – coal-mining, the
iron and steel industry, shipbuilding, engineering, and the textile
trades. Nor were the printing trades immune from such accusations.
In coal-mining, after giving geological difficulties their due, criticism
was decidedly apt. (See Table 6) In the iron and steel industry,
attention was occasionally drawn to the neglect of mechanical
charging and continuous rolling [8]. In shipbuilding, by the turn of
the century and even before, Britain's ancient reputation no longer
extended to the up-to-dateness of her shipbuilding techniques. Even
before the turn of the century, pneumatic and electric portable tools
for drilling and caulking were in fairly common use in American
shipyards. In British shipyards, the general use of portable tools,

TABLE 6

Percentage of Coal Cut by Machine, United Kingdom, Belgium,
Germany, and the United States, 1913 and 1926

Year	United Kingdom	Belgium	Germany	United States
	%	%	%	%
1913	8	10	2	51
1926	22	71	66	74

SOURCE: I. Svennilson, *Growth and Stagnation in the European Economy*
(Geneva, United Nations Economic Commission for Europe, 1954), p 110.

although neither entirely unknown, nor entirely neglected, was, in the
early nineteen-hundreds, still largely a thing of the future [9]. Yet
another instance of failure to adopt a mechanical device for handwork
as quickly as had the Americans is provided by type-setting. In the
United States, machine composition was 'rapidly supplanting typesetting by hand' as early as the eighteen-nineties [10]. The invention
was an American one, and the lead in installation was America's too.

Then there was the case of moulding. British foundries were slow to install moulding machines, or at least slow in realizing their full potentiality [11].

In the engineering industry (aside from moulding) and in the textile trades, it was not a question of lack of mechanization *per se*: machine shops, spinning mills, and weaving sheds left little scope for purely hand work at this comparatively late stage in the technological evolution of the two industries. Rather, in these industries the problem was that of slowness to adopt certain newly invented machines and mechanical devices to replace or supplement existing prototypes. For example, British machine-shop practice was behind American when it came to the installation of milling cutters. Moreover, British engineering establishments were apparently not making full enough use of the grinding machine – 'where great accuracy is required, grinding is unapproachable' [12] – for finishing operations [13]. In the textile trades there was the question of ring-spinning. Ring-spinning was exceedingly widely practised in the United States well before the turn of the century: in the eighteen-eighties and eighteen-nineties it was being rather indifferently received by a British industry still wedded to the mule [14].

Another trade that was occasionally scored for inadequate mechanization was the lock industry. The introduction of the American cylinder-type lock around the turn of the century was associated with a considerably greater degree of mechanization in the industry. Here, too, there was a noticeable disparity between English and American practice. Although British lockmakers were beginning to turn to the cylinder type early in the century, the lock trade of Britain was still being criticized for clinging too long to the old ways [15]. The furnishing trade and the joinery shop provide two final examples. The representative on the Mosely Commission of the Amalgamated Furnishing Trades' Association insisted that the American furnishing trade was much more mechanized than the British [16]. In joinery establishments, machinery had first appeared during the eighteen-seventies and 'eighties. In later years this development was furthered by an increased demand for ready-made doors, stairs, and other wooden items used by builders. But this was another instance of Britain's relative slowness to convert to a more mechanized dispensation. The representative on the Mosely Commission of the General Union of Operative Carpenters and Joiners felt certain that American manufacturers of joinery employed machinery to a much greater extent than was the case in Britain [17].

Among the more spectacular examples of late nineteenth-century technological 'break-through' were those few devices that embodied some form of the automatic principle. 'The modern development of the automatic principle is notably illustrated by machine tools and the automatic loom,' Shadwell observed in 1913 [18]. (The mention of machine tools should have been confined to the lathe.) To these, he might have added the Owens automatic glass bottle-making machine. As regards all three, the Americans led in both initial development and rate of adoption. The application of the automatic principle to the lathe was one of the outcomes of the continuing evolution of the turret and capstan machines, both of these devices being products of the machine shop revolution of the latter half of the nineteenth century. There is no doubt that the British engineering trades displayed a certain slowness in taking up the fully automatic lathe [19]. This was not a case of total neglect. The automatic screw machine – the device used for producing small threaded articles such as nuts, bolts, washers, and similar items 'from the bar' – was reasonably well entrenched in British engineering practice during the pre-war years. But the auto turning machine – used for work on castings and forgings of almost every description – was not adopted as widely as efficiency enthusiasts in the engineering profession would have liked. The enthusiasts were, however, willing to concede a reason for this shortcoming. Small threaded items of more or less standardized dimensions were constantly being demanded, so that the automatic screw machine never lacked conditions favourable to its employment. The auto turning machine, on the other hand, did not enjoy the same advantage of volume demand for standardized products. Add to this a relative lack of standardization in the engineering trades, and inadequate scale of operation and insufficient specialization of output on the part of individual manufacturers, and we have a setting which was not very favourable to the employment of automatic turning machines, or of any other fully automatic device, for that matter [20].

Whatever automatism there was in the cotton and woollen trades was to be found almost entirely in the weaving of cotton cloth. At the end of the nineteenth century, there had appeared in America an automatic loom, the Northrop, whose development had been the work of an English migrant to the United States. The Northrop loom made its first appearance in Britain early in the present century, but it was far less extensively adopted in Britain than it had been in the United States. True, the Northrop loom was at first not particularly well-suited for the weaving of the finer grades of cloth. But this cannot completely absolve Lancashire from the charge of complacency and obduracy when confronted by this important innovation [21]. The Owens bottle-making machine, another American invention, first came on the market in 1907. However, its manufacture and use soon became subject to the decisions of an international cartel which had purchased the original patent rights. The existence of this arrangement was no doubt partially responsible for the relatively slow introduction of the Owens machine into Britain.

The Pace of Production

Many of those who, sixty years ago, commented on the state of British industry harboured some sort of preconception concerning the tempo of British manufacturing industry and the pace at which things were done in comparable pursuits in other lands. Thus, the representative on the Mosely Commission of the Associated Iron and Steel Workers thought that the slabbing mills of America were operated at 'very quick speeds, quicker than any I have seen in this country' [22]. The leather workers' representative believed that 'machinery in the States is run at a higher speed than our own' [23]. Similar observations came from those students of industrial problems who were anxious to direct attention to the allegedly lackadaisical methods of British industry. Forty-five years ago, in his *The World of Labour*, G.D.H. Cole wrote that speeding up had gone 'much further in America than here; . . . the great growth of speeding-up in this country is recent, and has not yet had time to make its efforts felt' [24]. Two decades later, Burnham and Hoskins, anxious to exonerate Britain's iron and steel workers from the charge of adhering to a 'traditional' (that is, slow) pace of work, pointed out that high labour costs and relatively low labour productivity in the British iron and steel industry were primarily the result, not of proletarian sluggishness, but of the pace of production which had been set by the plant, and by those who owned, organized, and managed the plant [25].

But how to bring quantitative precision to bear on the question of operating speeds? In their replies to the query, 'How far is greater output in American factories due to – (*a*) Longer hours of work? (*b*) Greater speed at which the machinery is run?', the Mosely delegates were far from unanimous. The representatives of the ironfounders, iron and steel shipbuilders, weavers, and bookbinders refused to concede any American superiority in the matter of output per man. (We assume that this is what the 'greater output' of the query referred to.) The representatives of the blastfurnacemen, the Midland Counties' Trades Federation, the boot and shoe operatives, and the leather workers were of the opinion that the 'greater output' of American factories was due to both longer hours and greater operating speeds. Those who represented the cotton spinners, carpenters and joiners, and paper makers attributed the differential solely to faster speeds, while the representatives of the furnishing trades and the lithographic printers could find the cause in neither factor. The representatives of the Amalgamated Society of Engineers, the Sheffield Cutlery Council, the brick-layers, and the TUC's Parliamentary Committee thought that the productivity advantage was due to a higher degree of mechanization and more efficient organization. The evidence, therefore, was not entirely on one side, although the balance seemed to be in favour of faster operating speeds, to which, of course, must be added greater mechanization and superior organization.

Possibly there can never be a completely accurate reply, but some evidence can perhaps be gleaned from the *attitudes* of those who directed Britain's industrial machine to the so-called American tempo. In a leader on 'Intensified Production' in *The Engineer* in 1901 we read that

> ... intensity of production does not bear the stamp of antiquity; on the contrary, it is a thing of recent growth. Ten years ago it was not so much as heard of in the United States; the automatic machine tool as we have it now is a modern affair. It is only within the last five years that the work of manufacturing at express speed has been developed at the other side of the Atlantic. It is well known that working at this pace tells heavily on not only the workman, but every member of his staff; ... [26]

A welcome concern for the human cost of 'express speed', but does it also strike that same cautious note reputedly characteristic of the country's entrepreneurial and managerial community? Shadwell, too, opined that speed, like everything else, could be carried too far. 'Speed is not an end in itself,' he wrote in his *Industrial Efficiency*, 'and may be overdone or misapplied, like many other things. The object, from the point of view of industrial efficiency, is neither quantity nor quality in itself but a combination of the two in varying proportions according to the class of products.' [27] An admirable sense of proportion, provided that it is not allowed to degenerate into a bland acceptance of the *status quo*.

Electrification and the Electrical Trades

To some, the most 'deadly' instance of industrial–technical lag in Britain was that in respect of electrical development [28]. Others were inclined to take a less serious view. However, whatever the seriousness of this shortcoming, expressions of dissatisfaction with the country's electrical development were a commonplace. In the main, the criticism centred upon electrification for both driving and lighting purposes, although criticisms were also heard concerning electro-chemistry and electrical metallurgy. Thus, in the reports of the members of the Mosely Commission, inadequate electrification provided grounds for another of those Anglo-American comparisons unfavourable to Britain [29]. Among the industries frequently cited as being extremely slow to electrify were the textile trades and the iron and steel industry. Textile mill owners were taken to task by the author of an article that appeared in *The Engineer* in 1904 [30]. In the textile industry, if steam engines and their accompanying apparatus of wheels and belts for transmitting motive power could have been replaced by electric motors, the result would in many instances have been a marked increase in operating efficiency, including considerable economies in fuel consumption. But British mill owners were wed to the older source of motive power. The iron and steel trades came under fire in a paper delivered to the Iron and Steel Institute in 1902, a paper entitled, somewhat hopefully, 'The Application of Electric Power to the Iron and Steel Industries' [31]. In this industry, the focus of the criticism was on electric metallurgy rather than on the use of electricity as a source of motive power.

The electrical lag persisted a long time. Surely Clapham erred on the side of optimism when he wrote that 'by about 1905–10 . . . [this] deadly lag . . . was being wiped out' [32]. Certainly, the Report of the Departmental Committee appointed by the Board of Trade to consider the position of the electrical trades after the war [33] did not support the view that this shortcoming was being eliminated during the pre-war years. Indeed, the long subsequent history of inadequate electrification makes Clapham's view of the matter somewhat less than accurate.

As certain observers were quick to point out, various special circumstances could be pleaded in mitigation. To mention a few old chestnuts, there was the extent of Britain's capital investment in steam and gas, a deficiency of suitable hydroelectric power sites, and one or two legislative anomalies like the Electric Light Act of 1882 [34]. Here was more than enough, the argument ran, to delay the spread of electrification. But more important than all of these was the state of the British electrical industry itself. The indictment of the industry by the wartime Departmental Committee appointed to study it leaves little to the imagination. The industry was in a bad state. The spectacle it presented was that of an agglomeration of firms producing unstandardized items. The Committee held that there was only one route to 'a sound and permanent industry'. Not surprisingly, the recommended route was that of amalgamation, specialization, and standardization. It was a route which the industry, concentrated 'in the hands of a number of weak concerns', had manifestly failed to take [35].

Iron and Steel Technology

In the iron and steel industry, it was again the old story of clinging too long to outmoded practices. Possibly the outstanding example of obstinacy in the industry was the prejudice against the basic steel process [36]. The basic process, an English discovery (1876–8), was at first almost totally neglected in the land of its birth. This process could have considerable cost advantages over the older, acid process. The raw material for the latter was largely imported hematite. The basic process, on the other hand, could make use of domestic bodies of phosphoric ore [37]. It is true that, initially, the basic steel made from Bessemer converters was qualitatively inferior to the acid product. But it is also true that this quality advantage would disappear if basic steel were made in open-hearth furnaces rather than Bessemer converters. Although the open-hearth furnace eventually predominated in Britain as elsewhere (and, indeed, earlier in Britain than elsewhere) – by 1913 the volume of open-hearth production in Britain was almost five times greater than Bessemer [38] – the change-over to *basic* open-hearth steel was relatively slow, if the evolution of the industry on the Continent be the criterion. In the British industry, the prejudice against basic steel persisted long after consumers' doubts – even those of the slow-moving Admiralty – had been allayed by steel technologists both in Britain and abroad. The output of basic steel began to surpass that of acid only during the war and postwar years [39].

The bill of indictment against British iron and steel technology could include many other shortcomings: failure to organize on a sufficiently large scale coupled with a failure to carry far enough the physical integration of processes, a relative neglect of fuel economies, insufficient attention to electric metallurgy, and slowness to adopt continuous rolling. As to the first of these, it could be said that not only did old, family-owned [40] and relatively small-scale productive units proliferate in the British iron and steel industry, but far too few of these productive units, viewed as separate phases in series of related processes, were ever integrated into single, continuous operations, even when the units in question were within the same ownership complex [41]. Thus, to the critical eye, a much larger proportion of the industry's total productive effort should have been absorbed into those great vertical combinations which concentrate coking capacity, blast furnaces, and steel mills upon a single site or upon a number of immediately adjacent sites [42]. If a more integrated arrangement had become typical, a great deal more metal could have been passed from furnace to mill in molten form, thus avoiding much of the necessary but costly cooling and reheating of the metal. Moreover, assuming the installation of the appropriate type of coking oven, increased use of coke-oven gas for fuel would have been made possible. The location and organization of rolling mills provides still another instance of neglect of physical integration and co-ordination of processes, not only within the steel industry itself but between the steel industry and related industries. Thus, the location of rolling mills *vis-à-vis* shipyards, and, indeed, the total extent of the contact between the rolling branch of the steel industry and the shipbuilding industry, left much to be desired [43]. Nor did the geographical scatter of steel tube and pipe plants give cause for satisfaction [44].

As already intimated, significant progress in the matter of fuel economies might have been another consequence of a more integrated arrangement of productive processes, but such progress was also dependent upon an increased effort to deal with a variety of chemical, metallurgical, and mechanical problems, and a greater willingness to install those devices that were the fruits of progress in these fields. Thus, assuming a desire to integrate where it was advantageous to do so, significantly greater economies of fuel consumption could have been achieved if the industry had done more to install coking ovens of the by-product recovery type [45]. Gas from these ovens could have been combined with blast furnace gas, cleansed by the electrostatic process, to generate electricity for rolling mills. But here, as with other phases of iron- and steelmaking, British practice was far behind that of the Continent. As the Balfour Committee on Industry and Trade observed, 'These [by-product recovery] developments were to an important extent the result of German and Belgian research, and practice in this country with its cheap and abundant supplies of coal fell behind that of some continental countries in the matter of fuel economy during the years immediately preceding the war' [46].

Yet another instance of weakness lay in the field of electric metal-lurgy. In this respect, the British industry lagged considerably behind that of Germany. In Britain, steel produced by electric furnaces – electric furnaces are used, primarily, for the production of high-quality steels – failed to attain anywhere near the volume of output attained in Germany [47]. Much of this was probably another con-sequence of disregard by the industry of the need for continuing research in chemistry and in metallurgy.

Finally, there was the question of rolling techniques. Here the main charge centred on the continuous process. Continuous rolling afforded the advantage of increased operating speeds by eliminating that manipulation of the metal which was necessary between 'passes' wherever non-continuous rolling was still practised. Moreover, costs could also be reduced by the lower power requirement of the continuous process. Ironically, the continuous mill was another British invention, but except for wire-rolling it made little headway in the British industry, in sharp contrast to American practice [48]. Possibly the immediate roots of this shortcoming lay in the limited degree of standardization of rolled steel products in Britain [49].

Mention, too, might be made of an ancillary pursuit, the tinplate industry. When it came to electrification, mechanization, and general

up-to-dateness the great South Wales tinplate industry was un-
questionably behind the tinplate industry of the United States. The
representative on the Mosely Commission of the Associated Iron
and Steel Workers was particularly pointed in his criticisms of
British tinplate making.

> The tinplate works [in the United States] are all of a modern character
> . . . A noticeable feature is the strength of their mill trains and size of rolls,
> also the character of their engines. There is no such thing as 'stalling'
> throughout American mills. The engine power is always in excess of the out-
> side demands made upon it . . . One could not help contrasting this with the
> feeble and spasmodic grind at many of our own works . . . Electricity is
> used to a very great extent throughout their mills. Overhead electric cranes
> are in every works, by which rolls are changed in a few minutes, and sheets
> conveyed from place to place with ease and dispatch. Doubling shears are
> also driven by electric power . . . In cold rolling they are far ahead of our
> own methods by the use of tandem mills, the plates being conveyed from one
> set of rollers to the other on endless chains . . . Throughout their pickling,
> annealing, tinning and finishing processes, they are very much ahead of us in
> the nature of the appliances and methods of work . . . Overhead cranes are
> used throughout their annealing departments.

Then, as a kind of damning summing-up, he added that 'The tinplate industry [in Britain], like the sheet trade, is over-weighted with
obsolete machinery' [50].

3

Organization

What are the criteria of excellence in the matter of organizing production at the plant or firm level? It cannot be said that the logic of every industrial context demands maximization, in a crude physical sense, of division of labour, specialization, standardization, and scale of operation. A high level of efficiency necessitates the ascertainment of an *optimum* degree of specialization and standardization, and an *optimum* size of plant or firm. Other optima to be determined include those of plant layout and flow of production.

British performance with respect to any of these, during the period under consideration, left much to be desired. The principal industries of America and Germany – especially the iron and steel industries of those two countries – could have scored several points against their British counterparts in regard to most of the more desirable forms of organization of production. The problem had engaged the attention of members of the Mosely Commission. Some of their accounts of American practice in the matter of plant layout and the organization of production were most enthusiastic, and, implicitly or explicitly, denigrating of British practice. 'There is no doubt that the leading [steel] mills of American manufacture are far ahead of our own best mills in their arrangement . . .' This was the opinion of the representative of the Associated Iron and Steel Workers [1]. The representative of the London Consolidated Society of Journeymen Bookbinders admired the 'special attention that is paid to the arrangement of . . . plant' in the United States [2]. The representative of the Amalgamated Society of Leather Workers thought that the 'organization which exists in the workshops [in the States] is truly worth considering' [3].

To deal, now, with the particulars of these and similar observations.

43

Specialization, Standardization, and Interchangeability; the Mass Production Technique

Specialization as an element of the organization of production comprehends two distinct, although closely related, phenomena. First, there is that division of labour which, historically, split up productive processes within individual plants into a large number of new subdivisions. This tendency was accompanied by the invention of a host of specialized machines and machine tools. Moreover, subdivision of process also resulted in the splitting up of various trades and occupations into new occupations or craft entities. For example, the trade of the old-fashioned engineer eventually became the preserve not of one man but of a multitude of specialists. Secondly, specialization embraces the tendency for individual manufacturing units to specialize their outputs by narrowing the range and variety of products turned out.

During the closing decades of the nineteenth century and first decade of the present century, both aspects of specialization were becoming more common. Thus, contemporary students of industrial problems constantly commented upon increasing division of labour within individual manufacturing units resulting in the subdividing of productive processes and calling into being specialized machines and workers. And they also spoke of a tendency for these same productive units to turn to outputs of a more specialized nature. As to the first of these, or intra-plant division of labour, the annual Factory Reports, the Minutes of Evidence of the Poor Law Commission, professional journals such as *The Engineer* and trade union periodicals like the Amalgamated Engineers' *Monthly Journal* afford an abundance of relevant observations. In 1908, Sidney Webb declared for the benefit of the Poor Law Commission that 'speaking generally, occupations have become more specialized' [4]. Especially in the limelight, in this respect, were the engineering and boot and shoe trades. A leader in the Amalgamated Engineers' *Monthly Journal* for June 1899, which proclaimed that 'specialization is undoubtedly becoming the order of the day' [5], touched off a spate of correspondence on the question in which 'order of the day' is the recurrent theme. As to the related tendency, specialized production, we read in a paper to the British Association in 1907 that 'these are the days of specialization'. The author, a professional engineer, then went on to point out that 'manufacturers tend to specialise in one article as much as in one class of article' [6].

Yet, in spite of unmistakable trends in the direction of increased division of labour and specialization of production in Britain as elsewhere, British industry did not reach any remarkable level of achievement in regard to either of these. That British industry still had some distance to travel before it could boast of the degree of subdivision of manufacturing process that was reputedly characteristic of American industry was a matter to which more than one member of the Mosely Commission had adverted. The representative of the United Society of Boilermakers and Iron and Steel Shipbuilders declared that 'the system is adopted in America of dividing and sub-dividing mechanical labour to a greater extent than prevails in England', while the representative of the Associated Shipwrights Society observed that in America 'specialization of industry and sub-division of labour . . . are carried on to a much greater extent and with a minuteness which has not reached here . . .' [7]

Those who harboured misgivings over the extent to which British industrial undertakings specialized their outputs also had much to seize upon. Two key industries – engineering, and iron and steel – are cases in point. In the engineering trades, specialized production had, it is true, ceased to be an exceptional phenomenon, for the old-fashioned 'general machine shop' was gradually giving way to more specialized productive units making either single machines, single types of machines, or sometimes even single parts of machines. Yet, in important sectors of the industry, and particularly in component production, specialization had, during these years, still not been carried to the limits that the 'logic of industrial organization' required. Even in the West Midlands, where the new cycle and auto trades of Coventry and Birmingham could be regarded as possible stimuli to a high degree of component specialization, the response of manufacturers to these stimuli was not striking. The region abounded in a 'multitude of small independent producers [in the brass, screw, nut and bolt, paint, pressed-steel, tube, iron-founding, leather, spring, and plating trades] who could adapt themselves to the manufacture of motor parts' [8]. 'Could', but, to a considerable degree, did not (although there did emerge among them a number of component specialists catering to the needs of the automobile trade). As to specialization in the engineering industry as a whole, the indictment of the Committee on the Engineering Trades After the War is scarcely restrained.

> We have . . . been much impressed in the course of our investigations by the very large number of relatively small firms that exist . . . each producing a multiplicity of articles. Some of them seemed to take a special pride in the number of things they turn out; whilst few of them seemed to be willing to contemplate buying at a cheaper price a component part from a rival manufacturer, even if they were permitted to do so by that rival [9]

The Committee then drew the inevitable British–German–American comparison. In the two latter countries, 'the number of patterns produced in each works is strictly limited . . . One manufacturer may specialize on a certain article forming a part only of a completed product and other manufacturers requiring that part will buy it from him and cannot make it themselves'. In Britain, on the other hand, 'except in the cycle trade, there is practically no one to compare with the component specialist who exists throughout the United States' [10].

In steel rolling mills, product specialization was eminently feasible, given a sufficiently large productive unit. Either the entire mill could be devoted to rolling steel of a particular type and gauge, or the mill could be divided into sections, each section specializing in a different variety of product [11]. Either way, constant changes of rolls would be avoided and the possibility of achieving significant economies could then be brought within reach. But British mills were noticeably remiss when it came to specialization. The judgment of two of the industry's historians is severe but apposite. 'British [steel] plant was . . . general and adaptable, but not specialized.' [12] However, there was at least one good reason for this state of affairs. In the British industry the scale of operation was all too frequently inadequate. But there were other reasons as well [13].

Standardization on a nation-wide scale has never been one of the strengths of British industry. Writing in the early nineteen-thirties of the 'illogic' of manufacturing operations in many British industries, Professor Sargent Florence spoke of a 'myriad variety in the articles provided', and of the 'multitude of sizes, shapes and qualities of the same sort of article' [14]. This view of the matter, coupled with the usual unfavourable comparison with American industry, would have been even nearer the mark had it been made three or more decades previously [15]. Certainly, it had relevance to the engineering industry. It is true that many of the products in the engineering trades are not only complex in character but undergo never-ending changes in design, and hence are not ideally suited for sweeping schemes of standardization. Yet, according to the authors of the Report on the Engineering Trades After the War, a certain amount of standardization was both feasible and necessary. 'Whilst the over-standardization of patterns has a tendency to the stagnation of improvement, . . . a number of products in this country could, and ought to be, reduced to a common standard so that a needless variety of patterns should be, as far as possible, reduced.' [16] The Committee found much to deplore as far as actual practice was concerned. No 'two manufacturers seem intentionally to produce the same article, . . .' [17] Individual branches of the industry drew similar critical comments from other observers, the manufacture of railway locomotives being a case in point. In 1903, *The Economist* pointed to the relative absence in this sector of the industry of the degree of standardization which was apparently characteristic of the manufacture of locomotives in the United States [18].

Engineering was not the only industry to draw fire in the matter of standardization. In 1900 an anonymous complainant writing in *The Engineer* took the electrical industry severely to task for lack of standardization [19]. And complaints about the inadequate standardization of British electrical equipment were to be heard for many years to come.

Yet another important industry subjected to this kind of criticism was the iron and steel trade. When comparison was made with rolling practice in other advanced industrial countries, one could fairly conclude that the standardization of rolled steel sections in Britain had not been carried nearly far enough. As late as 1900, British-made steel sections conformed to no single system of dimensional standards, whereas steel sections had been standardized in Germany in 1883, in Belgium in 1885, in France in 1896, and in the United States in 1898. In Britain, however, the late 'nineties saw a mounting tide of criticism, emanating principally from those whose immediate gain lay in a reduction in the excessive number of different types and sizes of steel sections; that is, from merchants who with the increasing use of steel were anxious to cut down storing and marketing costs, and from certain producers who wished to avoid having constantly to change their rolls and (if these producers were vertically organized) to take advantage of the continuous process [20]. In 1901, *The Engineer* angrily noted that the 'heterogeneous nature of rolled sections has long been a bugbear to both makers and merchants . . .' [21] Others felt the same way. In 1901, the Engineering Standards Committee was born. Almost at once the Committee drew up a scheme for the standardization of steel sections [22]. Yet even after the Engineering Standards Committee had been in existence for more than a decade and a half, the Committee on the Iron and Steel Trades After the War could still complain that 'the sizes and weight of steel sections used in shipbuilding, bridge, and structural engineering are too numerous . . .' [23]

An important facet of standardization is interchangeability, or dimensional standardization of components. Waste and relative costliness ensues where machines and machine-shop practice are untouched by the interchangeable system and where assembly involves the 'mutual fitting of parts' [24]. Where interchangeability is the rule a set of parts forming a single machine does not have to be specially made for that machine, but may be taken at random from series of interchangeable replicas. Theoretically, a system of interchangeability or component standardization could be industry-wide, or even nation-wide, in scope. Common threaded articles machined to nationally observed dimensional standards were no novelty to the Britain of 1890. Sir Joseph Whitworth's proposals for a standard series of screw threads initially met with opposition 'in many quarters from those who thought that the maintenance of some particular form of screw-thread would ensure customers returning to them for repairs' [25], but eventually his system won widespread acceptance. However, with the exception of a host of common details such as screws, nuts, bolts, and similar items, which are made to conform to certain national standards of type and size, the usual sphere of interchangeability has remained, to this day, that of a single plant or firm. And, in the British industry of seven or eight decades ago, even systems of component standardization which were only plant- or firm-wide in scope were in large measure things of the future. The same observation applies to later decades, for machines made of components drawn from stocks of interchangeable duplicates could scarcely be said to have been a commonplace in 1900, or even 1914. (During the war, however, military necessity provided a considerable spur to the spread of the interchangeable system.) In a

48

paper on 'Modern Machine Methods' published in *The Engineer* in 1902, the author drew up a savage indictment when he wrote of 'the rubbish now sold', in regard to which 'the loss of even the simplest part necessitates the purchase of an entire apparatus, so little is interchangeability practised' [26]. This may have been overstatement, but surely the charge was not too wide of the mark. A year earlier, the president of the Institution of Mechanical Engineers had expressed the more moderate opinion that the interchangeable system had not been sufficiently widely adopted in Britain [27]. Even in the last edition of his *Principles*, Marshall was still writing that the 'importance of the principle of interchangeable parts has been but recently grasped . . .' [28] How 'recent' may be seen from the wondrous tones adopted by Lord Aberconway when he described the interchangeable principle in his *Basic Industries of Great Britain*, published in 1927.

> The engines and machinery produced by the Lincoln firms are made to certain types, the parts being numbered or lettered so that the customer in any quarter of the world, needs only to send the name and the number or letter of reference to Lincoln, to receive at once a duplicate which can be fitted by the driver or user of the machine. [29]

This shortcoming was the logical consequence of other deficiencies, in the realms of both organization and technology. As to organization, during the pre-war years and earlier, a greater dependence upon component specialists, at least in the newer branches of the engineering industry and certain allied trades, might well have conduced to increased standardization of parts and a more widespread practice of the interchangeable system. However, as we have already seen, such specialists did not achieve anything approaching a major role in the productive arrangements of the day, even where there was a most obvious need for them, as in the automotive, cycle, and some of the other newer trades of the Midlands.

As to technology, two of the technical props for an interchangeable system were somewhat underexploited in British industry prior to the war. The first of these was the limit gauge. The second was a pair of devices – the jig and the fixture. The part played by the limit gauge in furthering the spread of interchangeability, although not absolutely indispensable from a technical point of view, must nevertheless be considered extremely important when it came to realizing the full *economic* potential of the interchangeable system.

Interchangeability requires for its fulfilment certain standards of accuracy and precision of workmanship. But the accuracy required need not be of the 'dead fit' or absolute variety. And it was precisely because systems of interchangeable components required for their achievement not absolute accuracy, but merely the ability to turn out work accurate within certain tolerances, that these systems had important cost-reducing consequences. After all, working within prescribed tolerances not only expedites machining, but because it eliminates a great deal of the need for rectifying inaccuracies in pieces after they have been machined, speeds up the work of assembly as well. Then, too, because the need for old-style fitting can to a considerable extent be eliminated under an interchangeable system, so, too, can the skilled fitter. But these cost-reducing advantages might be partially nullified if the devices used to measure pieces being machined had to be micrometers, callipers, and the standard plug and ring gauge. The use of micrometers and callipers conduced neither to speed nor to the elimination of the need for skill. With the standard plug and ring gauge, limits of tolerance simply cannot be ascertained and 'dimensions are made in accordance with skill, judgment or experience of the workman' [30]. This is precisely where the advantage of the limit gauge lay.

With the limit-gauge system it is only necessary to determine what the allowable limits are to be and to then make use of a maximum and minimum gauge, by which sizes are kept within the prescribed limits . . . with these [limit] gauges comparatively unskilled labour will – aided by the proper out-fit – quickly learn to produce work accurate within limits of 0·0006 in. when using the external limit gauge and within 0·0016 when using the internal limit gauge. These limits are none too close for [some] ordinary engineering work [but] close enough for interchangeability, even in fine machine work. [31]

What, however, was the extent of the adoption of the limit gauge in the British industry of sixty years ago – at a time when it was already fairly well known and pleas for its use were frequently appearing in technical papers? [32] If the exhortations were many – the Engineering Standards Committee had set up a sectional committee to investigate limit gauges (among other things) [33] – so, too, were complaints of neglect. The author of the paper on machine methods that appeared in *The Engineer* in 1902 observed that 'although the "limit" gauge in certain firms has been in use for years, particularly among gun and small arms makers, it is surprising how little its advantages are known and understood by manufacturers for every-day work of all sorts' [34]. While it is true that this shortcoming was to a very considerable extent eliminated during the war when the need arose for 'repetition production' on a colossal scale, the fact remains that as late as the third year of the conflict the president of the Institution of Mechanical Engineers could complain that there were still shops – too many shops? – which were not as yet making use of limit gauges [35].

Jigs and fixtures provide another support for an interchangeable system. (The fixture holds the piece to be machined in place, while the jig, in addition to performing this function, guides the cutting tool to its exact position.) Without resort to a jig or fixture, the placing into correct position of a piece to be machined – for example, a casting or a forging – necessitates extremely careful setting by means of a chuck, clamps, and other instruments. But where it is desired to produce in quantity, the setting-up operation and 'locating' may be considerably simplified, and the time consumed in setting and locating greatly reduced, if a jig or fixture is employed. Moreover, these devices not only increased the speed of manufacture but they also furthered the displacement of skill in fitting or assembly. Like the limit gauge, therefore, jigs and fixtures enabled manufacturers to take advantage in practice of the various opportunities for cost reduction that the principle of interchangeability afforded in theory.

The jig was not new to the twentieth century. In America, Eli Whitney had made use of a kind of jig. Prototypes of modern jigs had also been employed in the manufacture of gun-locks and sewing machines after mid-century in both the United States and Britain. But what of the Britain of the early twentieth century? Numbers of *The Engineer* for the early nineteen-hundreds abound in articles extolling the virtues of jig work and urging upon manufacturers and engineers greater use of the jig [36]. In a paper on jigs and fixtures read to the Institution of Mechanical Engineers in 1914, it was claimed that 'at the present time there is no shop of any importance, specializing particularly in any class of work that does not go in very largely for jigs and fixtures' [37]. However, even as late as 1914 such a claim might not have been entirely accurate. Certainly it did not reflect the realities of a decade-and-a-half earlier. A leader in *The Engineer* for 8 February 1901, points out that although the use of the jig was not new in Britain at that time, these devices were not as yet really widely employed [38]. (The reason proffered was 'the peculiar condition of British trade' which militated against the adoption of the methods of repetition production on the American pattern and scale.) Probably the truth of the matter is that the use of these devices on a really wide scale had to wait until British industry began to feel the pinch of military necessity during the First World War. Yet, even as late as 1917, the president of the Institution of Mechanical Engineers maintained that in not a few sectors of British industry there was still a regrettably infrequent resort to jig work [39].

Specialization, standardization, and interchangeability are all components of the mass production technique. A simplified description of this technique is to be found in the phrase, 'standardised repetition work' [40]. There is of course more to mass production than these words suggest [41]. First of all, mass production obviously implies a large-scale operation. But to bigness and to standardization must be added specialization of plant and division of labour, mechanization and automatism – and each of these in a highly developed form. And in some of those instances where the mass production technique reached a very advanced stage, it culminated in the smooth, uninterrupted flow of the conveyor belt system.

How close had British industry come to the methods of mass production two generations ago? The manufacture of paper, from the middle of the nineteenth century on, had been characterized, to a degree, by 'uninterrupted flow' techniques. But paper is a simple product. Where the final product was more complex, comprising a set of component parts, very little that partook of the nature of mass production could be discerned, if we take as a criterion what had already been achieved by a famous American automobile manufacturer prior to the First World War. British practice in the same and related industries – or in any industry, for that matter – was a far cry from Henry Ford's achievement [42]. What little there was of the mass production technique was to be found in sectors of industry where the interchangeable principle could be applied. Traces of it can be discovered in the sewing machine and cycle trades, some of the newer branches of the engineering trades, and, to some extent, in the electrical trades. Yet, in spite of these beginnings, it was not until the First World War, when shells and other more or less standardized items were required in tremendous quantities that 'standardised repetition work . . . took the place [in many sectors of the engineering industry, and in other trades, too] of the varied and variable output, characteristic of such British manufacture before the War' [43].

Again, it must be borne in mind that the mass production technique and its principal components usually feed upon bigness. Typically, to have taken *full* advantage of specialization of output, subdivision of process, specialized machines and specialized workers, standardization, and continuous flow production required exceedingly large-scale production [44]. It will be recalled that in the case of steel rolling mills in Britain, a relatively small scale of operation was an important inhibiting factor as regards specialization. The same was true of various other industries that were slow to exploit the economies of specialization of output and subdivision of process. And the spread of standardization and continuous flow production were similarly encumbered.

Scale of Operation: Size of Plant and of Firm. Integration

It was no surprise, therefore, when the wartime inquisitors into the state of British industry found yet another weakness in the proliferation of small, separate productive units in areas of industry in which the optimum scale demanded large plants, and, in some cases, large firms enjoying various degrees of vertical integration of process as well. (Sometimes, the optimum size might call for horizontal combinations, too.) Two industries, possibly three – and key industries in any advanced economy – drew most of the fire. Thus, the Committee on the Electrical Trades drew attention to the existence in that industry of 'a number of weak concerns . . . dabbling in a variety of productions' [45]. Here consolidation was a must [46]. A charge of antiquated industrial organization, ill-suited to the needs of mass production, applied *a fortiori* to the iron and steel industry. Too many of the individual units, at the various stages of production, were too small for the attainment of a high level of operating efficiency. Even before the turn of the century, the productive capacities of the largest British blast furnaces and steel mills were being dwarfed by those of Britain's principal rivals abroad [47]. But the proliferation of relatively small-scale productive units was only one aspect of bad organization in this industry; insufficient vertical integration of these units was another. As has already been pointed

53

out, too many of the productive units in the industry (especially coking ovens, blast furnaces, and rolling mills) which should have been linked in series of integrated operations existed as independent plants.

In the engineering industry, the optimum scale of operation would naturally admit of a wide range of possible magnitudes. Yet here, too, there were complaints of a vast clutter of small productive units. Although the Committee on the Engineering Trades was not primarily concerned with problems of organization and scale of operation – technics of production and operational methods were given more attention – the question of size was nevertheless considered. According to the Committee, the task of setting the engineering industry's house in order must not stop at the installation of more efficient equipment: far too many of the country's engineering works needed to be laid out on a larger scale [48].

Thus, what was characteristic of the electrical, iron and steel, engineering, and other trades in America and Germany was much less characteristic of these same pursuits in Britain; and this in spite of the fact that there was in Britain a legal atmosphere which, unlike that of the United States after 1890, was relatively free from the more explicit kind of ban upon combination and collusive action hostile to the spirit of 'free competition'. On the other hand, it can scarcely be said that great integrated industrial complexes were entirely unknown in Britain. Moreover, there was no dearth of associative devices other than amalgamations or outright mergers. In fact, many a voice was raised in criticism of the alleged lack of vigorously competitive behaviour in British industry and of the tendency to seek security in price-fixing and other market-rigging arrangements. But this is part of another story.

PART 3

The Reasons

4

Management, Education and Society

The Quality of British Entrepreneurship and Management [1]

In connection with the organizational factors greatest prominence should be given to the skill of management in achieving and operating the best factory organization for the purpose. This includes a wide range of functions, such as planning of factory lay-out, the placing of the machinery, programming production, planning the flow of work and the interdependence of operations, planning the handling of materials, dealing with the question of supervision.

> L. ROSTAS, *Comparative Productivity in British and American Industry* [2].

In my humble opinion the fault does not lie with the British workman in the leather industry, but rather with the employer. He sticks too much to the old ideas. He does not keep pace with the times.

> From the report of the representative on the Mosely Commission of the Amalgamated Society of Leather Workers [3].

(*a*) SOME GENERAL CONSIDERATIONS

No industrial machine can be better than the minds that direct it. If the machine is antiquated and slow-moving, then the directing minds can frequently be shown to have been unreceptive to innovation.

Evidence of ineffective entrepreneurship and management in British industry can be found, but it scarcely admits of quantitative assessment. At any rate, contemporary opinions on the matter abounded. The members of the Mosely Commission had their attention directed to the problem when they were asked, 'Are [American factories] better managed?'. Of the intelligible replies, ten were in the affirmative and seven in the negative. (Four respondents did not seem to have any strong opinion, either way.) The following are typical of the affirmative replies: 'The American

57

manager is more enterprising and more ready to introduce the latest and best of everything' (G. N. Barnes of the Amalgamated Society of Engineers) [4]. 'American employers interest themselves in the management of their business to a greater and more intimate extent than is the custom in England' (T. A. Flynn of the Amalgamated Society of Tailors) [5].

Alfred Marshall had touched upon the problem both in *Industry and Trade* [6] and in the *Principles*. In the latter, there is the celebrated *obiter dictum* concerning the decline of entrepreneurial vigour in firms in which wayward sons, born to a life of ease, succeeded fathers who had carved out their niche through hard-headed diligence [7]. And the same sort of quasi-sociological observation recurs in the memorandum that Marshall wrote in 1903 on 'The Fiscal Policy of International Trade'. '[Many] of the sons of manufacturers [were] content to follow mechanically the lead given by their fathers. They worked shorter hours, and they exerted themselves less to obtain new practical ideas than their fathers had done; and thus a part of England's leadership was destroyed rapidly.' [8]

Although there is surprisingly little exploration of the problem of the quality of British management in Shadwell's monumental study of industrial efficiency, the author does not ignore it entirely. A 'prominent manufacturer' is quoted as saying that if Britain's industrialists have been 'outstripped' by foreign competitors, the 'greater part' of the blame lies with the 'manufacturer himself; he has been too supine and easy-going' [9]. A specific group singled out by Shadwell for want of enterprise were the employers in the cotton weaving trade [10]. Another critical note is struck by Shadwell in an article on 'The Welfare of Factory Workers' in *The Edinburgh Review* in 1916. This time, the criticism centred on knowledge of techniques and on planning.

[The] best disposition of mechanical processes between the material and the product can be determined by the methodical application of adequate technical knowledge. That is to say, a series of operations with a given equipment can be planned so as to give the best results. This is rarely done in a systematic way by British manufacturers. The number of works in which it is even attempted can be counted on one hand. Very often there is no planning at all; it is left to the operative and rule of thumb. Generally there is some planning of a rough and ready kind, but some of the most famous works in the country are in such a state of chaos that the stuff seems to be turned out by accident. [11]

Perhaps no contemporary observer of industrial matters dealt with the question of managerial efficiency in British industry more causticaly than J.A.Hobson. In his postwar volume on *Incentives in the New Industrial Order*, Britain's employers are made to answer to an indictment which, in places, is drawn in terms that are little short of violent. Finally, mention might be made of that series of articles on trade union malpractices ('The Crisis in British Industry') that appeared in *The Times* early in this century [12]. Digressing from his fulminations against unions to point an accusing finger at managerial indifference and ignorance in the printing trade, the author of the series (E. A. Pratt) wrote that 'There can be no doubt that the most serious cause of new methods and new machinery not being rapidly adopted is to be found in the general absence of accurate technical knowledge, both of the machinery itself and in the management of the men, on the part of the responsible chiefs of the majority of big printing houses' [13].

The hostile comments that Hobson and others directed against British entrepreneurs and managers are perhaps partially vindicated by leaders such as the following:

No journal not wholly devoted to the subject has given more attention to the question of automatic machine tools, which is intimately connected with latter-day systems; and we have never ceased to recommend their employ-ment if it could be fairly shown that, when all the conditions were con-sidered, an economy might be anticipated from their use. But a hasty acceptance of apparent improvements is to be deprecated. Because a machine has a large output it does not follow that it must be better econ-omically than one that produces less rapidly. Speed has to be paid for in some way or other. That is a fact frequently forgotten. You cannot get a greater output without using a more expensive machine or a more expensive man; . . . [14]

No irresponsible endorsement of the restless spirit of change this! On this matter, *The Engineer* no doubt reflected the attitudes and prejudices of a great many managers.

Managerial conservatism had also caught, and revolted, the eye of Sidney Webb. In a series of wartime lectures that he delivered to works managers [15], Webb chided his audience for what he consider-ed to be glaring instances of managerial ineffectiveness. Here, as elsewhere, the Webb ideal was the engine of efficiency and the achievement of nothing less than absolute perfection with respect to organization and planning. What Webb saw in the British industry as it actually was was far from perfect, even by canons of perfection less exacting than his own. To substantiate his criticisms he cited a recent presidential address to the Institution of Mechanical Engineers. The president of the Institution had declared in 1917:

> Except in a few cases, workshop organisation here has not received the attention given it in America or Germany. There are still shops without definite planning of the progress of the work, without adequate equipment of jigs and gauges, and without standard shapes of tools or a tool-room; where men drift about in search of tools or tackle, or wait in idleness for drawings and materials; where machinery is so obsolete and light so bad that good work cannot be done if the machinery were up to date. [16]

(b) A CASE STUDY IN MANAGERIAL ATTITUDES IN BRITAIN: THE RECEPTION ACCORDED 'SCIENTIFIC MANAGEMENT'

In developing his critique, the president of the Institution of Mechanical Engineers had not been entirely negative. He posited an ideal to work toward: the 'scientific management' of men like Frederick W. Taylor, Carl Barth, H. L. Gantt, and F. B. Gilbreth, whose ideas were beginning to receive fairly wide attention in the United States during the pre-war years. The American scientific managers claimed to have made a science not only out of job analysis, or the determination of the most efficient ways of laying out productive operations and (through time and motion study) of the most efficient movements to be used in conjunction with these operations, but also of bringing workers to confine themselves to these 'best' movements [17].

It has been said that scientific management, American style, met not so much with outright hostility in British managerial circles as with almost complete indifference [18]. Probably the truth is that both attitudes were to be found. Of the comparative lack of interest in the Taylor creed in Britain prior to the First World War, there can be no doubt. Neither can there be any doubt as to an occasional outburst of overt hostility. This is not to suggest that Taylor's message always met with a favourable reception in the United States. Although hostility to Taylorism in America was most pronounced in trade union circles, it was scarcely confined to these circles. Nor is this to say that in Britain the reception was invariably unfavourable. After all, Taylor did have his British disciples, and this even before the war.

What of the charge of apathy? The British trade and technical press, or at least the engineering section of it, may perhaps be taken as representative of a variety of managerial opinions. In 1895, Taylor delivered his first paper ('A Piece Rate System') to an audience of professional engineers in the United States. Even at this early date, he was something other than a complete nonentity in the United States. But in Britain, of the three leading engineering journals it was only *The Engineer* that took note of Taylor's paper [19]. When in 1903 Taylor presented his second paper ('Shop Management') to the American Society of Mechanical Engineers, the silence in Britain was even more deafening. By that time there were four important periodicals in the engineering field, but not one of them favoured Taylor's most recent paper with so much as a mention [20]. Nor was the Taylor system of management frequently discussed at the annual meetings of the institutions of professional engineers. In 1910, Taylor, together with two of his leading disciples, journeyed to Britain to attend the joint meeting of the Institution of Mechanical Engineers and the American Society of Mechanical Engineers. No member of the Taylor group presented a paper at the meeting, but Taylor participated in the discussion of H. I. Brackenbury's paper on 'High-Speed Tools and Machines to Fit Them'. It was an appropriate juncture at which to intervene in the proceedings, since ten years previously Taylor had, with Maunsel White, developed the first really successful high-speed tool steel. But on this occasion Taylor chose to speak on a 'far broader subject' than the art of cutting metals and the use of machine tools [21]. Then followed an exegesis on motion study and some of the other essentials of the Taylor system. Brackenbury, in replying to Taylor, reminded the latter that his (Brackenbury's) paper had not dealt with the subject that Taylor brought up, adding that he 'would . . . have valued any remarks Dr. Taylor might have made on tools and machines' [22]. Brackenbury did, however, mention 'in passing' that British machine builders were 'studying the movements of men very carefully' [23]. Some hint as to how widespread in Britain such 'careful' study – that is, motion study – was, is given in a pamphlet on *Scientific Business Management* published by the Ministry of Reconstruction in 1919. 'Little consideration has been given [to motion study] in this country' [24], the authors of the pamphlet observed, although they added that 'it has not been overlooked altogether, for some of its principles are being acted upon as common-sense laws' [25]. How characteristic was this elevation of 'common sense' to the status of scientific principle!

The pre-war period also seems to have been almost bereft of British treatises on scientific management. H.N.Casson, in the introduction to the second edition of his *Factory Efficiency* [26], claimed that his book (originally published in 1912) was 'the first practical exposition of Scientific Management that has been written by a Briton on British soil'.

On the other hand, it cannot be said that there was a total conspiracy of silence against the Taylor system in the management literature in Britain during these years. In the 1905 revision of his *Commercial Management of Engineering Works* [27], F.G.Burton gave a synoptic account of the essence of the Taylor system. Seven years later came the Casson volume. Shortly after the end of the war the Ministry of Reconstruction published its study of *Scientific Business Management*, in which, incidentally, the name Taylor is nowhere to be found. As to the periodical press, both popular and professional, during these years and especially after 1910, the Taylor group and scientific management were, as already indicated, accorded some mention on more than one occasion. This coincided with a greatly heightened interest in scientific management in the United States. In 1910, freight rate hearings held by the Interstate Commerce Commission prompted a great flurry of popular interest in the Taylor system in America [28]. The Traffic Committee of Commercial Organizations of the Atlantic Seaboard, a group of eastern shippers, had appeared before the Commission to oppose an application for an increase in rail freight rates. The shippers' counsel, Louis D.Brandeis, chose to berate the railways for inefficiently conducted operations, his *coup de grâce* being a reference to the principles of what he called 'scientific management'. Brandeis had consulted members of the Taylor group [29], and his advocacy of their creed before the ICC received very wide publicity [30]. The following year, Taylor published his first major treatise, *Workshop Management*, and in 1913 came his *magnum opus*, *The Principles of Scientific Management*. Widespread ignorance concerning Taylor's principles undoubtedly still prevailed in management and engineering circles in Britain, but various British technical and trade journals were at last beginning to take notice [31]. The reception was mixed, but opposition to Taylorism was a much more frequent reaction among British commentators than was espousal of the Taylor creed.

Certainly, neither of the two principal voices of the British engineering world – *The Engineer* and *Engineering* – were moved to active support of the Taylor system.

At least three separate strands can be found in the critical comment that was directed against the American scientific management movement in Britain. First, there was that criticism which sprang from humanitarian considerations: 'men and women are not machines' (although, conceivably, this might on occasion have been a mask for conservatism, or even wounded national pride). Another unfavourable reaction to Taylorism was grounded in some spurious reasoning in economics. There was not the same need for scientific management in the United Kingdom as in the United States, it was sometimes argued, since labour costs were not as high in the former country as in the latter. (Not the first time that labour costs have been confused with *wage rates*!) Finally, there was the critical note which smacked of both condescension – more shades of aroused nationalism – and the British 'pragmatic spirit' at its blindest: 'why all this so-called "science", when what is required is merely "common sense"?'.

Examples of all three types of reaction can be found in a variety of places. Thus, a leader in *The Engineer* of 19 May 1911, which dealt with the Taylor system in a decidedly hostile vein, wanted nothing in humanitarianism.

There is much to be said for, but in our opinion and in that of a great many American managers, more to be said against Taylorism. Everyone knows that it is labour that costs money, and that economising labour reduces production expenses more rapidly than any other practicable saving. But there are fair ways and unfair ways of diminishing labour costs ... We do not hesitate to say that Taylorism is inhuman. As far as possible it dehumanises the man, for it endeavours to remove the only distinction that makes him better than a machine – his intelligence. [32]

A leader the following April – 'Taylorism Again' – returned to the attack from the same vantage point. 'Taylorism is scientific management gone mad.' [33] Nor did this kind of hostility abate during the following year. A leader of 25 April 1913 was devoted to 'Scientific Management and Works "Efficiency"'. '[Too] much science and a too rigorous systematisation of method to the exclusion of all other considerations is likely to lead to a decrease of efficiency rather than an increase.' [34] But on this occasion the Taylor system is not considered to be an unmixed evil. The leader writer concedes,

There is this to be said for the movement . . . It has shown in many cases how much may be gained by a modified system carefully applied; it has shown the value of wise and sane management; and it must have shown to many observant men among workers how much their capacity for work may be increased and wastage reduced by careful regulation. It has, moreover, increased the value and importance of the central authority by putting it into closer touch with all the processes of manufacture.

On this note the compliment ends, for 'further than this [scientific management] cannot go beneficially . . . [In] the last resort the man is more than the system, whether he be manager or worker' [35]. A leader a few months later gave no indication that the editors had relented. 'At the back of the minds of [Taylor and Gilbreth] is the conception of a factory as a huge machine tool. They do not look upon men and women as men and women, but as many parts of the great machine.' [36] But *The Engineer's* hostility did not spring entirely from humanitarian grounds. 'There is not in the United Kingdom the same need to economise labour costs . . .' [37] Then, a note of condescension. Why grace these principles with the highflown designation, 'scientific management'? A common-sense approach to the problems of management is just as 'scientific', and of this there was presumably no lack in Britain.

[No] works manager would be worth his salt who did not endeavour ceaselessly to make his labour bill per unit of output lower. To call this scientific management is simply to give a high-sounding title to an old and well-understood thing. The manager who pulls out an old machine and puts in a new one, who takes down rope-driven travellers and erects electric cranes, who adopts automatic machinery in place of hand tools is, if you like to call him so, a scientific manager. But the epithet seems unnecessary . . . It is the ordinary doctrine of works that better methods must be adopted as soon as they present themselves. It is scientific, of course, but to call it scientific is like speaking of the common pump as a philosophical instrument. [38]

From *The Engineer* we may turn to what was to become, after successive editions, a major, if not the most important, British treatise on factory management. E.T.Elbourne's *Factory Administration and Accounts* first appeared in 1914 [39], but not one of the successive editions through which it ran refers to any member of the Taylor group by name. Still, the author does mention 'Scientific Management', but in an unfavourable light. In the 1914 edition, Elbourne explains that it is not *his* intention to provide 'golden rules' for achieving industrial efficiency [40]. This is the aim of the American scientific managers, but 'golden rules', or organization *per se*, 'can never be a substitute for good men . . . [While] proper organization ought inevitably to weed out the inefficients, it ought not to hinder the full exercise of the best qualities of the best man . . .' [41] Moreover, Elbourne continues, even granted the usefulness of certain scientific management procedures, such as the exact detailing in advance of operational sequences, not every works management could stand up to the rigours of such procedures [42]. Hence, the relatively limited applicability of these procedures in an industrial milieu in which 'not every administration is strenuous enough to achieve planned results day after day' [43]. *The Engineer* took the occasion of a review of Elbourne's book for yet another tendentious aside on those 'scientific management' ideas emanating from the other side of the ocean. Elbourne's work, it proudly announced, 'is *English* in its sentiments' [44]. On this occasion, however, *The Engineer* was willing to concede that scientific management methods *might* be applicable in certain areas of *American* industry. But in British industry the 'physical and social' conditions were hardly comparable [45].

Not surprisingly, various voices on the left joined the chorus of critics. To G. D. H. Cole, scientific management was a threat to 'industrial democracy' [46]. J. A. Hobson, in a paper on scientific management published in the *Sociological Review* in 1913, was appalled at the prospect of scientific management reducing 'the labour of the ordinary employee to an automatic perfection of routine' [47].

But to Hobson, scientific management had its brighter side too. He agreed that it served a purpose where the work in question was of an exceedingly routine nature [48]. Then, looking at that aspect of scientific management which involved the 'selection and adaptation of tools to the special conditions of the work' [49], his opinion could not have been more favourable.

> If a shoveller can shovel more material without greater exertion by using a particular shovel, the system which ensures his using this shovel is beneficial to everybody, assuming he gets some share of the value of the increased output. When we turn from a simple tool to elaborate machinery, it becomes evident that quantitative testing is capable of achieving enormous economies. [50]

Sidney Webb had even fewer reservations than Hobson. In his 1918 series of lectures to works managers, Webb reported enthusiastically on what he considered to be the chief virtue of scientific management.

[Its best] feature lies in its psychological influence on the management itself, in its insistence on the perfect organisation of the factory, use of the best machinery, consideration of the conditions of the greatest efficiency of each worker, prevention of any loss of time, and prompt application of labour-saving appliances. [51]

Webb did however add a caveat. Job study was 'all to the good . . . in so far as it has for its motive . . . the discovery of how waste of time or waste of effort can be prevented', but if it were used to drive the worker harder or to lower his piece-rates, or earnings, the worker would rebel [52]. To ensure a smooth transition to the better features of scientific management, not only should incessant driving of the worker be avoided, but the worker should be consulted through his shop stewards or through workshop committees [53].

The principal proponents of the Taylor system in Britain were, however, to be found not among left-wing polemicists or social scientists, but in certain entrepreneurial quarters. During the pre-war years, Taylor's principal disciple in the United Kingdom was Hans Renold, of the engineering firm of the same name. Addressing the Manchester Association of Engineers in 1913, Renold claimed, possibly with a view to allaying the misgivings of his listeners, that the Taylor system of scientific management was 'neither more nor less than common-sense tabulated and applied with tact and reason when facing the everyday problems as they arise' [54]. Another enthusiast among men of business was Edward Cadbury [55]. And a final instance of sympathetic interest in various aspects of scientific management is provided by the *Report of the Departmental Committee [on] . . . the Position of the Engineering Trades After the War*. In a section entitled 'The Efficiency Engineer', the authors regret the almost total absence of such individuals on the British scene, but look forward 'to the rise of some such class of adviser' for the engineering trades of Britain [56].

The Taylor system, with and without modifications, was, therefore, not entirely without its British advocates. However, to what extent did British industry admit of the actual practice of Taylorism, or any of its variants – we have already touched upon the question of the practice of motion study – during the years preceding the First

66

World War? Writing in 1917, an American expositor of Taylorism claimed to have discovered 201 instances of the application of scientific management in industrial undertakings [57]. Of these 201, only four were to be found in Britain. How accurate was this assertion? Edward Cadbury and Hans and C.G.Renold were members of firms that claimed to be dealing with management problems in scientific fashion. Cadbury, in a paper delivered to the Sociological Society in 1913, sketched in some of the details of what he must have considered to have been a highly efficient arrangement of manufacturing operations, an arrangement which, among other things, made room for a planning department [58]. Yet, what he described – 'we give the most careful attention to the planning out of the workrooms and the procuring of the most up-to-date machinery' [59] – appears almost flaccid in comparison to what had been propounded in Taylor's *Principles of Scientific Management*. C.G.Renold, in his contribution to the discussion of Cadbury's paper, took the line that the techniques of scientific management were not as new or as innovatory in British industry as many people had imagined.

For many years works jobs have been closely studied, workmen have been carefully selected, detailed instructions for doing work have been given, tools and appliances have been standardised, even 'functional' foremen – notably inspectors – have been used. The principles underlying these schemes have long been at work to a greater or less extent, though, generally not all in the same works. [60]

There was a grain of truth in this observation. Various management techniques which sprang from the same kind of thinking that animated the American scientific management men did secure a foothold in Britain prior to the war, especially in the engineering trades. Examples are to be found in the 'feed and speed' system and certain of the newer methods of payment by results, such as premium bonus. Where the feed and speed system was practised, special supervisors were employed to determine, and enforce, optimum speeds and feeds for cutting tools [61]. (The 'feed' is the rate at which the tool is moved laterally to fresh areas of surface to be machined.) The continuous eruption of trade union objections to the employment of feed and speed men bears witness to an increasing resort to such individuals during the early years of the present century [62]. The premium bonus wage incentive system, which was also gaining popularity during this period, was another speeding-up device [63].

Evidence of the extent of the adoption of the premium bonus system in the engineering and boilermaking trades – these were the trades in which premium bonus was most widely adopted – is to be found in the Wage Census for 1906. This showed that 9·5 per cent of the turners (other than brass), approximately 8 per cent of the fitters and erectors, and 7·3 per cent of the brass turners, fitters, and finishers in the engineering and boilermaking trades were employed on premium bonus. Altogether, according to the Wage Census, some 4·8 per cent of the adult males employed in the engineering and boilermaking group, in 1906, were on premium bonus [64]. In 1909, the Trades Union Congress set up a joint committee to investigate the prevalence of the premium bonus system and, also, trade union attitudes to the system. As to its prevalence, the Amalgamated Society of Engineers reported that in 1907 over nine per cent of its 98,000 members were 'working on the bonus system' [65]. Other unions that reported experience with premium bonus included the United Machine Workers, the Moulders' Amalgamated Union, and the United Society of Boilermakers and Iron and Steel Ship-builders [66].

But the spread of premium bonus and similar schemes forms a slender basis from which to argue that a revolution in management techniques had swept over British industry during these pre-war years, or that the purer forms of Taylorism began to enjoy a secure foothold in Britain [67].

(c) THE ROOTS OF ENTREPRENEURIAL-MANAGERIAL SHORTCOMINGS IN BRITISH INDUSTRY

If it be granted that the quality of British management left something to be desired, why was this so? Are the answers to be found in social-psychological phenomena such as conservatism or a surfeit of caution, and in socio-cultural factors such as a deification of amateurism, a relative neglect of science, an anachronistic attitude to the training necessary for a career in industrial management, and a social structure which reserved too much of the room at the top for those who had arrived by the route of nepotism or class advantage?

(i) *The Conservative Blend*

The story of receptivity to change in British industry is, in large measure, the story of the impact of innovation upon an essentially conservative industrial élite.

[It] is certainly a common belief that American industrialists are always more ready to scrap industrial equipment than are their British counterparts. This may be due to capital being more readily obtainable in the United States, but it may also be due to a psychological difference between the adventurous employers of the United States and the more conservative British employers. [68]

A disappointed professional engineer who delivered a paper on 'Double-Cutting and High-Speed Planing Machines' to the Institution of Mechanical Engineers in 1911 lamented the luke-warm reception that had apparently been accorded these devices in Britain [69]. An equally disappointed discussant observed that 'it was wrong to seek the reason for the non-adoption of double-cutting planing machines in the existence of mechanical defects in the principle. The reason really lay in the intense conservatism which permeated the whole engineering profession' [70].

One ingredient of the conservative blend was simply undue caution. Thus, a cautious Shadwell, commenting upon the Platt Brothers' textile machinery factory at Oldham, wrote that, 'The management is fully alive to the necessity of keeping abreast of the times, but it does not believe in "scrapping" machinery which does not work well, merely because it is old. There is undoubtedly a *via media* in this matter, and the restless pursuit of novelty for its own sake may be carried too far' [71]. Possibly in no sphere of industrial technique and organization was proneness to excessive caution among British entrepreneurs and managers more manifest than in the matter of scale of operation. Here the caution (or scepticism?) centred upon alleged economies of scale. Sir Lowthian Bell wrote to the Royal Commission on the Depression of Trade and Industry of his doubts concerning 'the economy of striving after excessive production in point of quantity' [72]. He was not merely balking at 'excessive' production at a time of recession or at blind adulation of size. He was expressing the same sort of sentiment that guided numerous entrepreneurs whenever they thought about scale and the purported economies of scale.

The conservative attitude was, however, not only a matter of undue caution. Sheer inertia, excessive confidence, and complacency were also apparent [73]. Thus, when manufacturers boggled at the large capital outlays necessary for the adoption of new techniques, was their hesitancy always grounded in prudence, in the wise refusal to take 'an important step forward ... until a certain quantum of prospective advantages [had] accumulated' [74], or was it sometimes rooted in an unwillingness to disturb the peace of a comfortable, secure position? Or did the hesitancy – and indifference – of owners and managers on such occasions also feed upon stubborn self-confidence and its attendant complacency?

How did the two latter arise? Did they constitute one of the prices the country had to pay for past industrial greatness? Marshall had alluded to the matter in his memorandum on 'The Fiscal Policy of International Trade' [75] when he wrote that, after all, it was not so very long ago that Britain 'had the ... benefits of railways' to an extent which no other country at the time enjoyed [76]. Fortunately also for Britain, the American Civil War, and Prussia's series of wars that began in 1864, not only kept two potential rivals out of the international economy, but, in addition, generated enlarged demands for British railway plant, textiles and other materials of war and peace. To Marshall, one consequence of this was a surfeit of self-confidence and complacency. Past greatness had made 'many of the sons of manufacturers content to follow mechanically the lead given by their fathers' [77].

Complacency had many manifestations, but to some of those who pursued this theme the principal sign was an abysmal lack of interest among industrial leaders in science and research, and in scientific training.

(ii) *The Cult of Amateurism and the Neglect of Science*

Because of the 'comparative intellectual ease with which the fabric of British capitalism [had] been built up', the country's 'great business men' appear to have carved out their niche in the world without the aid of either science or 'trained brains in others'. This was J. A. Hobson [78]. Continuing in the same vein, Hobson ruefully observed that 'energy and industry many [of our businessmen] possess, but it is very wastefully employed because of their contemptuous scepticism of science and all that science stands for ...' [79] Hobson was not alone. Others, too, had dwelt upon the allegedly widespread abjuration of science in British industry.

It was the munitions crisis of 1916 which, more than anything else, provided the target for those who had been carping at a variety of shortcomings in British industry, neglect of science being not the least of these. In 1916, a group of scientists and others – they did not have official sponsorship – convened a Neglect of Science Conference in London [80]. Speaker after speaker rose to express dissatisfaction with what was apparently considered *the* Achilles' heel of British industry. Alfred Marshall, who had been unable to attend the conference, sent a letter to the chairman expressing his conviction that England could not 'maintain her position in the world, unless she calls science to her aid in a much more thorough way than hitherto' [81]. Others were of the same opinion. Significantly enough, more than one of the conferees conceded the excellence of Britain's achievement in the pure sciences. The great trouble, so it was alleged, was the insufficient application to industry of the fruits of pure science. 'We have in our country competent experts in all the sciences . . . [The] difficulty is that they have not been appealed to': this from a professor of zoology at Oxford [82]. 'Our pure scientists, I think, hold their own in the world . . . It is rather in the greater application of science to industry where we have fallen short': this from a past president of the Iron and Steel Institute [83]. Inevitably, comparisons were made with Germany, a self-confident amateurism in Britain being contrasted to the emphasis on 'organised scientific work' in Germany [84].

It was especially in the application of chemical knowledge that inadequacy was felt. Again the pure scientist could be exonerated: Britain's achievement in this science stood second to none. However, there was no cause for adulation when it came to the British achievement in creating new industries and products from the growing store of chemical knowledge, or when it came to applying this knowledge to existing industries by employing trained personnel. In Britain, 'we tried to start chemical industries practically without chemists' [85]. Sir James Dewar, in his Presidential Address to the British Association in 1902, had placed the number of chemists (graduate and non-graduate) employed in British industry at 1,500 ('a very liberal allowance') and the number in German industry at 4,000 [86]. The Royal Commission on Technical Instruction of 1882 had not painted quite as bleak a picture as this. For example, it had pointed to the fact that most of the country's major metallurgical works employed chemists and had some sort of chemical laboratory for testing materials. But, unfortunately, 'these chemists were employed not as applied scientists, as researchers, that is, but as routine testers and analysts. The true applied science laboratory had not yet emerged in England; but it had appeared on the Continent' [87]. Even Sir Lowthian Bell, who usually found the way things were done in his and other British industries a source of pride, admitted to the Royal Commission on the Depression of Trade and Industry that 'he was not sure whether chemists of the higher class are not more frequently met with on the continent of Europe than in British establishments' [88].

(iii) *Social Mobility, Class Attitudes, and Recruitment for the Top*

One lesson that America has, with some justification, claimed to have taught the rest of the world is that although a high degree of social mobility is not an indispensable precondition for effective entrepreneurship and a high level of industrial efficiency, relatively fluid class lines can nevertheless provide a useful support for a continuing condition of entrepreneurial alertness and technical progress. In Britain, this support was more or less absent. A class-ordered society, undisturbed by a great deal of inter-class mobility, was, of course, not unique to Victorian and Edwardian Britain. There was as much deification of status in Germany. But in Germany, partially offsetting the rigidity of class lines, was an exceedingly widespread dedication to the ideal of rigorous scientific and technical training for those who would enter the key positions in the industrial hierarchy. In Britain, on the other hand, the consequences of social immobility and a too highly developed class consciousness up and down the social scale were not mitigated by widespread acceptance of the need for sound training for future industrial leaders. In Britain, therefore, social stratification could be viewed as a potentially serious obstacle to the development of entrepreneurial and managerial skills [89].

Of course, no accurate measure of social mobility or of degree of accessibility to the uppermost rungs of the ladder lies ready to hand [90]. But pertinent qualitative observations on the matter abound. Certainly, it was not merely captious criticism to have alleged that, 'Hitherto the higher professions have been the preserves of a small fraction of our upper and middle classes, with a thin precarious trickle of boys coming up from that section of the working class families able and willing to give a chance to a child of exceptional ability to win school prizes' [91]. Hobson might well have added industrial management to the 'higher professions' when he lamented the 'thin precarious trickle' which was the masses' contribution to the upper reaches. Critical comments were also to be found in rather unexpected places – for example, in the great debate, during the early years of the present century, over the existence of trade union restrictive practices. Writing in the *Economic Journal* in 1902 on 'The Printing Trades and the Crisis in British Industry', G. B. Dibblee insisted that, '[We] have not the same level of ability to draw upon for our employing class . . . as in the newer country [America]. The capable man rising from below has much greater difficulties in his way, difficulties which are the result of centuries of prejudice and class interest' [92].

The problem of recruitment and class prejudice was not solely a matter of negligible movement upward. The Establishment had traditionally not been favourably disposed to sending its own sons into industrial careers. '[The] best brains of our upper classes will go anywhere but into industry – into a bank or a merchant's office perhaps, but not into horny-handed manufacture.' [93] And, to step down the ladder a rung or two, members of the middle class were apt to acquire the same sort of prejudice, once they had absorbed the mores of their social betters. 'The attractions of dignified and cultured ease, of politics or the learned professions are too dazzling for that increasing class of people, those with small independent means.' [94]

Scientific Training and Technical Education – Another Case of Neglect?

If entrepreneurs were muddling through, heedless of the applied sciences, or were failing to employ people with the appropriate kind of training, did the fault lie in gross undervaluation, on the part of the owning and directing classes, not only of the right kind of education for those of their employees who held responsible positions, but for their own kind as well? Hobson was convinced of this.

Though every great modern business bristles with problems of high intellectual as well as practical moment, physical, financial, and administrative, how many responsible heads of business in this country possess any expert training in mechanics, finance, economics or psychology? The very notion of the need for such training appears to almost all of them a ridiculous pandering to intellectualism which unfits men for a real business life. Though a few of them are intelligent enough to recognize that Germany has got ahead of us in some profitable trades by employing scientific experts, and that the higher business training of young Americans is consistent with a rapid, lucrative career, very little has been done to secure for our industries the fruits of expert thinking and training. [95]

Over a half-century before this was written, the same problem had attracted the attention of Matthew Arnold. His *Higher Schools and Universities in Germany* (1868) made the sort of unfavourable comparison that was to be dinned into the ears of a later generation by Hobson, Lyon Playfair, Fabian Ware, J.N.Lockyer and others. In British industry, there was too much rule of thumb, too much 'blunder and plunder' (Arnold), and too little scientific education.

Critics who flailed British entrepreneurs for turning a blind eye to the need for proper training were of course opening up a much larger question. Were the *facilities* that were available for such training entirely adequate? Complaints about educational and training facilities were indeed frequent. They were directed, in the main, to three areas of alleged deficiency. First, as to the very top level – that is, the university and higher polytechnic institute – it was argued that the trouble was quantitative rather than qualitative (although some critics were inclined to speak disparagingly of the quality as well). Secondly, it was contended that the curriculum of the schools, including the great public schools, was too thin on the side of the sciences. At least this was the contention of those delegates to the 1916 Neglect of Science Conference who passed a resolution that 'the natural sciences should be made an integral part of the educational course in all the great schools of this country, and should form part of the entrance examinations of the Universities of Oxford and Cambridge as well as the newer Universities' [96]. Thirdly, that heterogeneous assortment of characteristically British institutions that range from day and evening schools offering technical instruction to artisans, to technical institutes just below the degree level received its share of criticism as well. The severest comments, however, seem to have been reserved for the reputedly inadequate number of institutions at the upper levels of this array.

As to the facilities available for intended skilled artisans and industrial workers of a lesser order of skill, opinion varied. Some of the witnesses who appeared before the Royal Commission on the Depression of Trade and Industry were critical, but on quantitative rather than qualitative grounds. The number of institutes was lamentably few relative to the need, so it was alleged [97]. It was also alleged that management was indifferent to this shortcoming. In this connexion, the following exchange between a member of the Commission and a witness who manufactured electro-plate and Britannia metal is instructive:

... might I ask what trouble, you, as a manufacturer, have taken in respect of teaching your apprentices; how are they taught and what system is adopted with regard to teaching them?

My apprentices ... get no technical education whatever except what they learn in the factory. There are schools of art in Sheffield, but the apprentices will not go to them; their masters do not care about sending them and they do not go; and as to technical schools there are none, so that practically they are not advancing at all. [98]

On the other hand, when comparisons were made with Germany entirely the opposite point of view was frequently heard, surprisingly enough. Thus, although it was usually conceded that German primary and secondary education had the edge in the matter of preparing the child for an industrial future [99], it was at the same time claimed that Britain led Germany as regards special technical education facilities for the worker [100]. Especially a matter of pride was the evening institute. The Royal Commission on Technical Instruction of 1882 found 'to their surprise' that the facilities available in Britain for evening instruction in science were unmatched anywhere else in Europe [101].

But, again, it would seem that the further up the technical education ladder one's critical eye ran, the less grew one's reason for satisfaction. Concern over the lack of physical facilities for instruction in 'higher technology' (and, also, over the relative neglect of the facilities that were available) was expressed on several occasions. The 1908–9 report of the Board of Education placed the blame on the country's employers.

The slow growth of [institutions for higher technology] is ... in the main to be ascribed to the small demand in this country for the services of young men well trained in the theoretical side of industrial operations and in the sciences underlying them. There still exists among the generation of employers a strong preference for the man trained from an early age in the works, and a prejudice against the so-called 'college-trained' man. [102]

Many of those existing institutions that were able to provide the proper kind of training stood idle 'in the daytime through lack of students' [103]. Cardwell points out that precisely the same complaint was made by the Board of Education in every annual report, right up until the outbreak of the war [104]. On the other hand, the entrepreneurial community can scarcely be accused of being uniformly indifferent to higher education and the role of higher education in an industrial setting. After all, some of the provincial universities and colleges that were established prior to 1914 – and this applies especially to Birmingham, Bristol, and Sheffield – owed their foundation, above all, to the initiative of members of the local business community. Still, to acknowledge the efforts in this direction of Joseph Chamberlain in Birmingham, of the Wills family in Bristol, of Mark Firth in Sheffield, and of men of business elsewhere, is not to exonerate British employers from the charge of being relatively indifferent to the need for *making use* of graduates of universities and institutes of advanced technology.

A Low-Wage Economy and Technological Backwardness – A Social *Problem in the British Context?*

It has often been argued that 'high' wage levels provide a stimulus to the installation of labour-saving devices and hence to technical advance generally, whereas 'low' wage levels can be a positive drag upon technical advance. The empirical support for these assumptions is usually drawn from international comparisons, as, for example, in Professor Habakkuk's recent study [105]. In the United States, money (and real) wage rates were higher than in the United Kingdom. About this there is little room for debate. But may the *usual* argument concerning the relationships between labour supply, wage rates, and technological advance be applied to these countries? That is, is it correct to maintain that just as a relatively scarce labour supply and high wages were a cause of capital intensity and labour-saving technological advance in the United States, an abundant supply of labour and relatively low wages were among the causes of the persistence of labour-intensive productive operations and a slow rate of technical change of the labour-saving variety in Britain [106]? In brief, that part of the argument that relates to American experience seems to be more plausible – except in one particular, to be examined later – than that which relates to Britain [107].

Still, acceptance of this relationship as it applies to Britain was (and is) exceedingly widespread. On more than one occasion, students of industrial problems in Britain pointed to an alleged sequence of low wages, low capital–labour ratios and technological lag. Dibblee, writing on the 'crisis of British industry', described how 'in England the employers in comparison [with those in America] are apt to attach too much importance to low money wages [whereas in America the employers] aim at securing efficiency of labour and less at low money wages . . .' [108] But was slowness to innovate in a labour-saving direction solely the result of this emphasis? A British employer, commenting upon 'problems of modern industry' at the close of the war, wrote that 'Before the War, it often happened that it did not pay to introduce labour-saving devices, because, apart from the difficulty of raising fresh capital, the interest charges came to more than the cost of cheap manual labour' [109]. For some who took this line, the coal industry was the example *par excellence*. In this industry, it was alleged, increasing real costs were the result not only of having constantly to tap less accessible, thinner, and more undulating seams, but also, in part, the result of neglect of mechanization where machine-cutting was practicable. This neglect could ultimately be traced, so the argument ran, to the continuing ability of mine-owners to recruit to the trade at wage rates that did not provide a spur to mechanization [110].

Was slowness to innovate in a labour-saving direction solely the result of relative factor prices? It can be argued that the *root* of the matter was not entirely economic. In the nineteenth century, the 'lump o' labour' fallacy of the working classes had as its more sophisticated counterpart among employers and writers on economic matters one or other variant of the wages fund theory. The important point, however, is that the kind of economic analysis which had produced successive variants of the wages fund principle was in part the product of a climate of opinion not inhospitable to class-dictated views concerning the 'just price' for labour. More specifically, the just price in this instance was a kind of *social* norm, or norm which must always be reconcilable with one's position in the social scale. Impliedly, then, a controversy concerning wages or piece-rates might turn upon a social rather than an economic norm or maximum. Indeed, even to this day, management in Britain has sometimes been heard to observe, during the course of an industrial dispute, that '£X per week is a quite high enough wage', implying that the norm or maximum is, or should be, *social* rather than economic [111].

This view of entrepreneurial attitudes in Britain might have been close to that of the man of business who sponsored the British trade union delegation to the United States in 1902. 'In England it has been the rule for generations past that as soon as a man earns beyond a certain amount of wages, the price for his work is cut down . . .' [112] Granted that the motivation to reduce piece rates was most frequently economic. But the 'certain amount of wages' might also have been a social as well as an economic maximum. If so, it sprang from a widely held attitude to social hierarchy – an attitude which, to say the least, was not conducive to technical progress.

A Note on Working-Class Morale and Psychology, and Technical Progress

Rigidity of class lines and (partially socially-determined) low returns to effort doubtless affected aspiration levels. If it be conceded that the socio-economic goals of the working classes in Britain were lower than those of their American compeers, might not this have had some effect upon the receptivity of British workers to innovation? And, does it follow that the work atmosphere of a society which stresses, and rewards, initiative and adaptability will induce a perpetual open-mindedness to change? Admittedly, this is problematical, but such a work atmosphere might at least abate the hostility that is ordinarily generated, because of fear of unemployment, by attempts to introduce new devices or new work methods. This is not to suggest that the industrial labour force of the United States was entirely pliant or wholly submissive in the face of innovation. But when a comparison is made between British and American working-class attitudes to technological and organizational change, a difference in degree becomes apparent. It is reasonable to assume that the latter derived in part from the different effects upon aspiration levels of the social milieux of the two countries. Becoming inured to the business of 'knowing one's station' does not conduce to constant upward revision of one's material goals, nor does it help to allay fears of technological unemployment. 'It is not that the objective factors (better lay-out, longer runs, planning of work, etc.) cause the [American] operative to work fast, but rather that those factors *enable the [American] operatives to fulfil their one clear object, namely to earn as much as they can,*' [113] – that is, *can* enable them to fulfil their object because social barriers in the way of this fulfilment are relatively absent.

The Labour Force, Trade Unions, and Innovation in Industry

The Accusations

Of all the reasons cited for Britain's supposed industrial lag, that which aroused the greatest controversy centred around the allegedly restrictive practices of trade unions and their members, and of the working classes generally. The case against labour rested, in the main, upon three supposedly proven charges. (The prosecution's brief included other accusations as well.) First there was the charge of outright opposition on the part of the working classes to mechanization, and, specifically, to the displacement of hand by mechanical processes. Secondly, there was the accusation concerning restriction of output. Finally, there was the charge of interference with the managerial prerogative of choosing the right man for the job by attempting to enforce archaic apprenticeship rules and to confine various processes solely to skilled operatives.

The first accusation, that of outright opposition to mechanization, was directed not so much against trade union leadership as against the rank and file. In the series of articles that appeared in *The Times* in 1901 and 1902 on 'The Crisis in British Industry', the Sheffield cutlery trades are cited as prominent cases in point [1], and a group of forge workers are excoriated for objecting to the introduction of electric cranes [2]. Shadwell, too, was attracted to the problem. He pointed to file-making and to the automatic loom as further instances of worker opposition to mechanical advance [3]. And these same two pursuits were singled out for mention by witnesses who had appeared before the 'Tariff Commission' [4]. Evidence heard by the Royal Commission on Labour and, later on, by the Poor Law Commission includes more than one allegation concerning worker opposition to mechanization. In a written reply to one of the Labour Commission's queries, a worsted manufacturer claimed that labour-saving machinery 'always meets with opposition from our hands' [5], and a tin plate manufacturer lodged a similar complaint [6]. A Newcastle-on-Tyne alderman who appeared before the Poor Law Commission maintained that the 'glass trade of the Tyne was absolutely ruined' because workers in the industry had resisted the introduction of machinery [7]. It would seem, therefore, that when the Webbs wrote in their *Industrial Democracy* that complaints against trade union opposition to machinery had disappeared, they were not being entirely accurate [8].

These allegations did not remain uncontested by trade union spokesmen and others. One of the Mosely delegates – the representative of the National Federation of Blastfurnacemen – maintained that he had 'never met with any objections to labour-saving appliances' in his trade [9]. Earlier on, similar denials had come from some of the trade unionists who had appeared before the Labour Commission. A witness who represented the Belfast Typographic Society before the Commission strenuously objected to any suggestion that members of his union had obstructed the introduction of typesetting machines [10]. The witness representing the Amalgamated Union of Manchester Bakers declared that he positively welcomed mechanization, since mechanization eliminated much of the very heavy work [11]. This witness's enthusiasm for mechanization was shared by the General Secretary of the Boot and Shoe Operatives' Union: machinery was a boon to his union because 'it increased the number of men required to make the work' [12]. And several of the Mosely delegates had reacted enthusiastically to the examples of advanced mechanization they had observed in the United States [13]. One wonders how representative of rank-and-file attitudes this enthusiasm for increased mechanization actually was.

Still, the authors of *Industrial Democracy* managed to disinter only two or three instances of outright rejection of machinery: the resistance that was apparently still being offered by the pearl button and stud workers of Birmingham [14], and by the file and table-blade forgers of Sheffield. The Webbs might have added to their list. Thus, Mosses, in his *History of the United Pattern Makers' Association*, records this union's 'unique experience', in 1898, of hearing a complaint from its Woolwich Branch over the introduction of surfacing machines in patternshops [15]. (The executive committee turned a deaf ear to the protest.) The evidence heard by the Labour Commission contains at least two instances of the old-fashioned kind of hostility to machinery (although neither instance was, on the surface at least, a case of outright rejection). The representative of the Amalgamated Society of Salt Workers proposed a tax upon 'labour-saving machinery' [16], a proposal which was also supported by the Secretary of the Dublin United Trades Council [17]. Yet another instance of the old hostility to mechanization is to be found in the Proceedings of the 1913 Trades Union Congress. 'On ... 7 July [the Financial Secretary to the War Office] ... received representatives of the Amalgamated Society of Farriers who desired to urge upon the War Minister the necessity of encouraging the industry of hand-made as against machine-made horseshoes.' [18] On the other hand, the Board of Trade's Annual Reports on Strikes and Lockouts for the decade-and-a-half 1900–14, yield only two instances, both of them relatively unimportant, of strikes which arose because of an apparent rejection of mechanical processes. In 1902 there was a strike of tailoresses in Limerick against the introduction of button-holing machines. It was not successful, for the work was 'resumed on the employer's terms' [19]. And in 1913 the Board reported a strike of Dublin bottle makers who were attempting to force their employer to abandon the use of bottle-making machines. Again, the employers won [20].

Probably the truth of the matter is that outside a few isolated pursuits, of peripheral significance in so far as the economy as a whole was concerned, old-fashioned, outright rejection of machinery was a rare occurrence. Two of the employers' representatives who had appeared before the Labour Commission – a boot and shoe manufacturer, and the secretary of the North and North-East Lancashire Cotton Spinners and Manufacturers' Association – testified that there had not been any employee interference either with the introduction of machinery or with improvements to existing machines [21]. 'The boot and shoe trade has been revolutionised in late years by the introduction of machinery, and that has been accomplished with the help of the unions'; thus a contemporary observer not altogether favourably disposed to trade unionism [22].

On the other hand, it cannot be said that mechanization was invariably greeted with enthusiasm by ordinary workers and union leaders alike. Hostility was deep-seated among various groups of workers – groups far more significant than the little fighting bands

of farriers and Sheffield file-forgers. An outstanding example is
provided by the typesetters and their attitude to the new Linotype
machine. Even those leaders who acquiesced in increasing mechanization (and surely they constituted the majority) did not always
accept a new mechanical device entirely without reservations. 'Do
you think it is a disadvantage to the country that there should be new
machinery, which may, and was intended to reduce the amount of
labour required?' a member of the Royal Commission on the
Depression of Trade and Industry asked James Mawdsley of the
Amalgamated Association of Operative Cotton Spinners. Mawdsley's
reply was guarded: 'I think it is an advantage, as increased production is required, and the old machines are worn out, that the new
mills should have new machinery, but to go on more rapidly than the
demands of the trade require, I think is a disadvantage.' [23] Yet,
withal, trade union leadership – again excepting archaic effulgences
of anti-mechanization – could hardly be described as Luddite. The
following is more or less representative of the kind of pronouncement
on the question of mechanization that union leaders were wont to
make in public. Addressing Congress in 1907, the TUC's President
warned that 'we can no more keep back the spread of machinery
than Mother Partington could keep back the tide with her broom' [24].
Caution, and perhaps even some hostility, might colour their utterances, but their strategy was a far cry from total rejection. In essence,
it was one of insistence upon various safeguarding provisions. This
was especially true of engineers, typesetters, and other groups of
organized workers who were having to confront new machines and
processes during these years.

The second accusation, that having to do with restriction of output,
provoked a great deal of acrimonious debate. It was restriction of
output which drew from the author of 'The Crisis in British Industry'
his vitriolic best. That there was evidence for its existence cannot be
gainsaid.

There were two principal manifestations of restriction of output.
First there were those stratagems and devices for restricting the
physical volume of production by limiting the input of human
effort. These included the notorious, but sometimes exceedingly
subtle, 'ca' canny' or 'go slow'. Secondly – these were much more
readily detectable – there were attempts, often stamped with the

approval of trade union officialdom, to restrict the number of machines that could be operated by a single worker. But whatever the outward form, restriction of output was usually rooted in the same kind of preconception: the old 'lump o' labour' idea, or the belief that the amount of work to be done or the amount of employment available was an unchanging entity to be divided carefully and equitably among the members of the labour force [25]. A more rapid rate of production resulting from technological advance might diminish the individual worker's portion of the aggregate 'lump o' labour'. Where piecework or some other system of payment by results was the rule the motive was somewhat different. Here we refer to the desire to prevent a downward revision of piece-rates consequent upon the introduction of a new machine or process.

This is not to suggest that 'ca' canny' or attempts to limit the number of machines per operative were prompted solely by technical change, or some change in methods or rates of remuneration. Fear of unemployment could always provoke a tendency to restriction.

'Ca' canny', and more overt forms of restricting output, appeared to be exceedingly widespread [26]. Certainly, there is no paucity of allegations. Employers representing the iron and steel industry contended, for the benefit of the Departmental Committee on the Shipping and Shipbuilding Industries After the War, that 'labour restrictions on output' were rife in their trade [27]. The authors of the *Report . . . [on] the Iron and Steel Trades After the War* singled out specific cases of restriction of output in this industry [28]. In the steel industry, the adjustment of piece-rates following the introduction of a new piece of equipment prompted further accusations concerning the practice of 'ca' canny' [29]. Nor were allegations wanting concerning the practice of 'ca' canny' in the engineering trades. 'Nearly every employer who appeared before us,' the Departmental Committee on the Engineering Trades After the War reported, 'had the same story to tell . . . The first complaint was that the workman deliberately restricts his output below that which represents a reasonable day's work . . .' [30] In shipbuilding and marine engineering, both the author of *The Times*' series and the Departmental Committee on the industry's postwar position added to the flurry of accusations [31]. The boot and shoe trade, the glass industry, typesetting, and coalmining provided further instances, or alleged instances, of 'go slow' [32]. But it was in the building trades, apparently, at least according to some of the accusers, that 'ca' canny'

83

and similar devices were most deeply rooted by virtue of tradition and, also, by virtue of the nature of the productive processes involved. 'In no branch of industry', wrote the author of 'The Crisis in British Industry', '. . . has this principle of restriction of output been more generally adopted than in that represented by the building trades . . . Not that the rules of the men's societies prescribed any such policy. It is a question of unwritten law . . .' [33]

Many, including some of the accusers, were inclined to exonerate the official trade union movement, and certainly the leadership of the movement, from the full force of the accusations. G. D. H. Cole, admittedly a committed observer, was quite categorical in his denial of the charge that trade unions and their leaders encouraged 'ca' canny' 'Ca' canny . . . is not countenanced in any Trade Union rule or bye-law or in any collective agreement that I have been able to discover . . . Ca' canny, so far from being one of the recognized devices of Trade Unionism in this country, is always met by fiery denunciation from the leaders of Labour.' [34] Lord Askwith – probably as unprejudiced a student of labour problems as it is possible to find – wrote that restriction of output 'appears to be applied more by the men than by the unions' [35]. In this, he is supported by G. Binney Dibblee. Writing in the *Economic Journal* in 1902, and apparently anxious to controvert the author of *The Times*' articles, Dibblee supports the position later taken by G. D. H. Cole.

> [It is often said that] labour organizations are to blame for keeping back the proper output of their members, and a great deal of evidence has been collected, especially in a series of articles in *The Times*, to prove the existence of a subtle conspiracy labelled 'ca' canny' pervading unionism and encouraged by its leaders, whereby a given quantity of work can be distributed to as large a number of hands as possible. Now we all know what 'making work' means. Every employer knows what it means; every one who has ever employed a plumber can imagine what it is like. But the accusation that 'making work' has been adopted as a system by unionism in general and that trade-union leaders encourage it I maintain is not proven, and moreover it is not true. [36]

Even the author of *The Times*' series, for all his vitriol, conceded that 'prominent' union leaders do not encourage 'ca' canny' openly, although he felt constrained to add that union leaders 'do so tacitly, and their subordinates, "shop delegates", and others, do so directly' [37]. As to the public utterances of union leaders themselves, the author of *The Times'* articles was unable to cite a single instance of advocacy of going slow. Actually, some of the union leaders were outspoken in their denial of official union support of restriction of output. Thus, George Barnes of the Amalgamated Society of Engineers, while acknowledging some inclination to go slow among the rank and file, refuted the idea that such an inclination was fostered by the union [38].

Accusations and denials aside, was there any *incontrovertible* evidence available of the practice of 'ca' canny', with or without official union approval? In the furniture industry, indirect evidence of the existence of 'ca' canny' can be gleaned from one of the collective agreements in the industry. In 1914, the Scottish Furniture Manufacturers Association and the United Furniture Trades Association revised Clause 2 of their 'Conditions of Settlement' to read: 'There shall be no restriction or undue pressure imposed on the time output of the workmen . . .' [39] But were there extant any union rules or collective agreements that actually prescribed restriction of output? G. D. H. Cole reported that he could not find a single instance of such a prescription in rules or bye-laws. Nor could he discover any in collective agreements. The author of *The Times'* series, however, cited the following, supposedly taken from the district bye-laws of the Friendly Society of Ironfounders of England, Ireland, and Wales.

Rule VII: Should any member of these branches consider that any of their shopmates are doing work in less time than it has taken formerly to do, whether set work or day work, or if piecework, doing for less money than the amount previously paid for the same pattern, it shall be the duty of each and every member in the shop to warn such member or members of the consequences attending the same . . . [40]

D. F. Schloss, in his *Methods of Industrial Remuneration*, claimed that more than one union had output-restricting rules – the Associated Shipwrights Society is cited as an example – and that similar provisions could be found in collective agreements [41]. Even G. D. H. Cole later conceded that 'in a few cases' (for example, in that of the compositors) there are rules which 'regulate the distribution of a limited amount of work so as to afford work for all' [42].

In the end, one is left with the impression that although a policy of deliberate go slow or limitation of output was by and large not part of the credo of official trade unionism, the rank and file were not altogether immune from the attractions of such a policy.

Like 'ca' canny', attempts to fix the ratio of machines to men also resulted in a continuing flow of recriminations. *The Report* ... [*on*] *the Iron and Steel Trades After the War* alludes to a 'marked tendency to insist upon the retention of as large a number of men as possible, when new machinery has been introduced ...' [43] Employers who made such accusations were not dealing with an entirely imaginary situation. G.D.H.Cole cites the following injunction from the rule book of the Associated Blacksmiths' and Ironworkers' Society: 'Rule 24: No member of the Society shall work more than one fire. Any member violating this instruction shall be fined £1 for the first offence, and for the second offence shall be liable to be expelled from the Society.' [44] The 1898 agreement between printing employers, including newspapers, and compositors in London contained the following provision: '[Composing] machines may be employed on Morning Papers in the day-time, provided that three case hands are called into each Machine, and that not more than three Machines are thus employed. [45] Explicit limitations on man–machine ratios in union rule books or in collective agreements, in other industries, were probably exceedingly rare, but the practice itself was not entirely so. In fact, the practice was a fairly common cause of dispute in the engineering trades, and other trades were similarly afflicted. In 1908, a group of striking weavers at Hyde had the machine ratio as one of their grievances. (The device in question was the Northrop automatic loom [46].) And the Board of Trade's annual reports on strikes and lock-outs record instances of similar disputes for other trades and other years [47].

The third major complaint, that having to do with the recruitment of labour to industry, was also directed at both workers and the official trade union movement. From management's point of view the matter at issue was whether or not employers should have complete freedom to employ any suitable person, whether properly qualified or not in union eyes, for any productive process. Pitted against this point of view were several major unions, adamant in their refusal to countenance the admission of unqualified – which to the unions usually meant unapprenticed – workers to the trade.

The trends to increasing mechanization, specialization, and division of labour of course exacerbated the issue, for all of these tendencies were reducing skill requirements in a variety of occupations.

Not only was there a diminution in the need for sheer manual dexterity, but the demands on the operative's intellect diminished, at least in those instances where such functions as tool-making, tool-setting, and the working out of operational procedures were transferred from the man at the bench to various specialists. In short, a number of industry's doors were being opened to a growing throng of lesser skilled and unskilled workers, male and female, adult and juvenile.

The issue was a particularly bitter one in the boot and shoe trade and in the engineering industry. During the eighteen-eighties and 'nineties the boot trade became a factory, machine industry, characterized by a considerable degree of division of labour and subdivision of process. New classes of highly specialized operatives came into being – operatives from whom were demanded exceedingly narrow ranges of skill – and the need for the craft skill of the old-fashioned bootmaker was relegated to the 'quality' sector of the trade. In the engineering industry, the skilled personnel were, largely for technical reasons, never driven into an insignificant haven for craft skill. They remained an important component of the industry's labour force, and they continued to dominate the industry's major union. Nevertheless, in the engineering industry the introduction of new machine tools and the perfection of older devices along more automatic lines radically altered skill requirements and generated demands for large numbers of relatively unskilled workers. The lathe is a case in point. With the increase in the volume of so-called 'repetition work', the old engine or centre lathe began to give way to more automatic prototypes, including the various types of turret and capstan lathe. Provided that the 'setting-up', often a highly complicated procedure, was done by a skilled man, an unskilled worker could after only a few weeks' or sometimes after only a few hours' instruction tend one of these newer lathes [48]. In many instances the manning of automatic and semi-automatic lathes became entirely the preserve of such individuals – 'machinemen' or 'handymen', as they came to be called [49]. Another development in the machine shop which had skill-displacing effects was the tendency to deprive machine tool operators (both skilled and unskilled) of the responsibility for determining correct feeds, speeds, cutting angles, and similar operating variables, and to make these the preserve of 'feed and speed' men or other specialists. The fitting shop, too, witnessed a measure of skill displacement when the continuing development of machine tools

87

designed for precision work resulted in a diminution in the need for the old-fashioned skilled fitter. To the extent that they were adopted in Britain – as we have had occasion to observe, there was admittedly neglect here – the limit gauge, jig, fixture, and systems of interchangeability further reduced the need for skilled fitting. Thus, much of the work of assembly became the preserve of a new class of semi- or unskilled erectors.

Among the unskilled workers in the engineering trades were to be found boys, women, and even girls. The employment of boys was a frequent subject for comment in the reports of the Amalgamated Society of Engineers' Organizing District Delegates [50]. Female labour in the industry was rather more exceptional, especially in heavy engineering and the other older branches of the industry.

And the army of the lesser skilled in the engineering trades grew in importance, both absolutely and relatively [51]. An entirely accurate measure of this tendency during the pre-war years is not possible, but if the postwar trend shown in Table 7 is extrapolated backwards, some notion of the magnitude of the problem during the earlier period may be had [52].

TABLE 7

Skill Composition of the Engineering Labour Force,
United Kingdom, 1914–26

Year	Approximate percentage of		
	Skilled	Semi-skilled[a]	Unskilled
	%	%	%
1914	60	20	20
1921	50	30	20
1926	40	45	15

[a] Largely machine-tool operators.

SOURCE: Committee on Industry and Trade, *Survey of the Metal Industries*, p 152.

In shipbuilding, too, a succession of technical changes (around the turn of the century, and before) had affected skill requirements. The more conspicuous instances of displacement of skill in this industry were the consequence of the introduction of portable pneumatic and electric riveting, caulking, and drilling tools. These devices could be placed in the hands of relatively unskilled workers [53]. In the printing trades, on the other hand, the issue was not so clearly drawn. In typesetting, the displacement of hand processes by the Linotype and Monotype did not result in a near-complete elimination of an old craft skill. The precise nature of the change in skill requirements was not beyond dispute. In any event, typesetting by machine became and remained a skilled occupation. Turning to the pottery trade, here we have a classic example of mechanization and the entry into an industry of workers, including females, whom the unions did not regard as fully qualified [54].

It was this intrusion of unskilled workers into various British industries that prompted the more powerful of the craftsman-dominated unions into frantic efforts to hold the line by attempting to force employers to accept the union view that every new machine or process, no matter how negligible the skill required, should remain the preserve of skilled operatives. In the engineering trades, the rise of the various classes of unskilled or semi-skilled machinemen was the cause of continuing strife. Certainly the 'manning of machines' question featured prominently in the Amalgamated Engineers' journals and reports for these years. The crux of the matter was the refusal of the Society and its kindred unions to agree with employers that any adult or juvenile who was given specialized training of relatively brief duration should be permitted to man machine tools such as turret lathes, planers, shapers, and slotters, and certain of the milling and grinding machines. In spite of their official surrender on the question in 1898, and again in 1907 [55], the unions continued to proclaim the right of the 'full-rated' (that is, qualified) man, as against the 'cheap man' or semi-skilled intruder, to work all manner of machine tools (except perhaps drills). 'The Machine question . . . in one form or another is so frequently cropping up . . .', complained an ASE Organizing District Delegate in 1901 [56]. '[The District Committee is] face to face with one of the most serious problems we have to deal with at the present, viz., the manning of machines,' reported the Liverpool Organizing District Delegate in 1902 [57]. 'I have interviewed a firm at Nottingham on the vexed question of manning of machines, and they use the usual argument of "No skill required", etc., and . . . the same thing was being done at other shops in the town . . .' [58] The same kind of dispute plagued the fitting shop where the skilled fitter was, as we have seen, having to confront a growing influx of semi- and unskilled workers. When it came to erecting, or the work of assembling without rectifying inaccuracies, the skilled fitter's position was hopeless. Even with respect to genuine fitting, he was constantly having to face competition from the ubiquitous 'handyman'. 'We waited upon the firm of R. Broadbent and Son ... to protest against a cheap man doing fitting and erecting ...' reported the Amalgamated Engineers' Organizing District Delegate for Manchester in 1913 [59]. The incident was scarcely an isolated one.

What, then, was the path of wisdom, from the union's point of view? If it became impossible to keep unskilled intruders out of the trade, should the union attempt to organize them? In 1892, the ASE decided to admit to its ranks all 'full-rated' skilled tradesmen, whether or not they had ever served an apprenticeship. But the semi-skilled and unskilled machine minder was still excluded from membership, and, of course, the employment of such individuals was not to be countenanced. Open warfare against the employers over this issue had failed in 1897, and most of the skirmishes since that time had also ended in failure for the union. When the machineman question was aired at the ASE's 1901 delegate meeting a different tack was taken. On that occasion it was decided to create a new class of members, the 'Machinists Section'. Machinemen were to qualify for admission to this section provided that they had been employed at their trade at least two years and were earning seventy-five per cent of the skilled turner's standard rate [60]. However, it was not made obligatory for the individual branches to enforce this decision. The branches could, if they so desired, continue to enforce the old admission rules. Not surprisingly, the new provision remained, to a very considerable extent, a dead letter. By 1904, only 4,000 members had been admitted to the machinists' section [61]. Nevertheless, in spite of apparent rank and file opposition, a delegate meeting in 1912 decided to throw the Society's doors open to almost everyone employed in an engineering shop by establishing a new section (Section F) for labourers, helpers, and others whose skill was of the lowest order. The new section did not last long: it was abolished in 1917. In any event, the decision to bring within the union completely unskilled workers had been practically inoperative, so hostile were the branches to implementing it [62]. The skilled man, then, continued to form the bulk of the Amalgamated Engineers' membership, and continued to dispute the 'rights' of employers in the matter of recruitment to the trade.

The pattern shop did not provide as much opportunity for the employment of unskilled men as did the machine or fitting shops. Yet even here a degree of mechanization enabled employers to make some use of lesser skilled men, which, in turn, provoked the usual reaction from the skilled employees involved [63].

The principal union in the shipbuilding industry, the United Society of Boilermakers and Iron and Steel Shipbuilders, was also having to cope with problems of skill displacement as a result of the introduction of new power tools. Its policy was the same as that of the ASE: keep the trade for the skilled man, technological change notwithstanding. But the union point of view in this industry did not always prevail, to judge from the number of disputes that arose in shipyards and boilershops over the employment of handymen and others on portable power tools [64].

The two unions that organized the compositors were both organizations of skilled men. Whether or not the Linotype machine actually displaced skill was open to question, but the compositors' unions took no chances. They both adopted the policy of confining the operation of these machines to their own members, on their own terms [65], with, it may be added, a high degree of success. Both unions signed agreements with the employers' associations that made specific provision for the training of their members for the machine process and, also, for the recruitment of machine operators from among members of the unions. However, as regards the latter, the ban imposed by the agreements was not absolute, 'preference' for their members being the maximum concession that the unions could extract [66].

One of the skilled man's traditional protective barriers against unskilled interlopers had been the apprenticeship system. Increasing mechanization and subdivision of process had two effects upon the old apprenticeship system. First, in those instances where a trade became a highly subdivided, factory–machine industry, as in the case of the boot and shoe trade, a regular apprenticeship practically disappeared. Secondly, where some semblance of apprenticeship – either indentured [67] or unindentured – remained, but where technological change and division of labour took their toll of skill requirements, apprentices often became little more than boy labourers [68]. Where this was the case, employers frequently attempted to increase the apprentice–journeyman ratio beyond what had been permitted by the custom of the trade or collective agreement.

Understandably, then, rigid adherence to a specific apprentice – journeyman ratio remained a common policy of unions still trying to use apprenticeship as a protective device in the face of innovation, skill displacement, and invasion by the unskilled [69], and hence provided additional damning evidence for those who sought to demonstrate that it was trade union obstructionism that prevented the country from reaping the full benefits of technological advance.

To some, the indictment against British workers and their unions should have extended beyond the three main charges. At least one of these other accusations cannot be ignored, since the alleged practice was doubtless one of the mainstays of the union position *vis-à-vis* innovation. Here we refer to attempts to protect wage rates and/or earnings in the face of technological change, or to preserve what the Webbs called the 'Standard Rate'. No doubt the distinction between rates and earnings levels was frequently blurred when the method of remuneration was piecework or some other form of payment by results. In any event, instances of strikes over the announced intention of employers to adjust piece-rates, consequent upon the introduction of some new device or work method, were countless. Scarcely a year passed without the Labour Department of the Board of Trade recording in its *Annual Report on Strikes and Lock-outs* some or other instance of disagreement over wage rates or piece prices following a change in work methods or the introduction of some new machine or product. (The vast majority of these disputes occurred in the textile trades.) The unions' determination to protect piece prices often resulted in attempts to bring within the scope of collective bargaining the matter of piece-rates revision. The efforts of the cotton operatives met with considerable success.

Any change whatsoever in 'the internal economy of the factory, or the manipulation of the workmen by the employer' is, in the cotton industry, referred to as matter of course for prior deliberation and agreement between the expert salaried officials of the Trade Unions and the Employers' Association. As the basis of negotiation, the principle of maintaining intact the Standard Rate of payment for a given quantity of effort is unreservedly accepted by both sides ... [The employers] agree, without demur, to a Piecework List ... The Trade Unions of cotton operatives actually meet the innovating employers half-way, by agreeing to a piecework rate which decreases with every rise in the productivity of machinery. The employer

92

therefore knows that every improvement that he can introduce will bring him a real, though not an unlimited, saving in his cost of production. The operatives, on the other hand, have the assurance that the graduated piece-work rates, already settled by mutual agreement, after careful consideration by their expert officials, will not only protect their present weekly earnings, but will also remunerate them for any increased effort involved. [70]

Sometimes it was the employers who took the initiative in having inserted in a collective agreement provisions for piece-rate revision in the event of technological change. Thus, the 1894 wages agreement between a North-East Coast shipbuilding employers' association and the United Society of Boilermakers and Iron and Steel Ship-builders contained a provision to the effect that the employers 'are to be entitled to a revision of rates on account of labour-saving machinery . . . The terms of these revisions [are] to be adjusted by a committee representing employers and the Boiler Makers' and Iron and Steel Ship Builders' Society' [71].

The Actual Core of Trade Union Policy vis-à-vis Technological Change

Once the more tendentious accusations against working people and their unions, and, also, the more obviously mendacious statements in defence of the unions, are eliminated, it is not difficult to see what it was that constituted the core of trade union policy with respect to technological change. Unions of skilled workers could not be accused of being unyieldingly or aggressively 'anti-machine'. Whatever the initial reaction of the rank and file to innovation, the official policy of the skilled workers' unions was, typically, one of defence. Acquiescence might be grudging, but the policies and stratagems actually adopted were far cries from outright rejection. It was simply a matter of defending, in the face of innovation, the preserve – or, as some might put it, the monopoly – of the skilled worker, and, also, of protecting his standard of remuneration (again allowing for some confusion between piece-rates and earnings levels). The skilled man must not be displaced by the untrained interloper, and the level of remuneration of the skilled man must not be jeopardized by any new machine or process. Hence the repeated insistence by trade union leaders on the right to determine, or at the very least to participate in the determination of, the conditions under which a new machine or process should be introduced. Thus, the

93

typical dispute prompted by the introduction of a new machine or process was not over mechanization or innovation *per se* but rather over the question of the *conditions* which were to surround the operation of the new device [72]. 'We have no reason to object to new tools; we only claim the manipulating of them where our work is concerned,' wrote a harassed ASE official to his executive committee in 1902 [73]. And when in 1907 the President of the TUC informed delegates to Congress that as regards mechanization the 'proper course to adopt is to recognize the inevitable', that is, acquiesce in new machines and methods, 'and concentrate energies on securing the best possible wages on working the machines' [74], he was merely enunciating another of the essentials of union policy.

The old attempt of the handcraftsman to exclude the machine has been definitely abandoned [by trade unionists]. Far from refusing to work the new processes, the Trade Unionists of to-day [c. 1897] claim, for the operative already working at the trade, a preferential right to acquire the new dexterity and perform the new service. In asserting this preferential claim of continuity of employment, they insist that the arrangements for introducing the new process, including not only the rates of wages but also the physical conditions of work, are matters to be settled, not solely by one of the parties to the wage contract, but after discussion between both of them.

This was the Webbs' view of the trade union position [75]. The burden of proof lies with those who would dispute it.

An Assessment of the Role of the Trade Union Movement, and of the Labour Force, in Britain's Industrial Development

If it be conceded that trade union policies and trade union attitudes were primarily of a job-protective and wage-protective nature, and were decidedly not Luddite in character, can it also be argued that the trade union stand and trade unionism *per se* were not in the least obstructive as regards technical and organizational advance? Even though union policies with respect to technical change were far from universally successful, the mere fact that they were considered by both leaders and rank and file as essential to everything the trade union movement stood for, especially in the case of the skilled workers' unions, might have been sufficient deterrent to innovation in some instances. And of course wherever employers who installed new devices that could be manned by unskilled personnel acquiesced

94

in the union position on the employment question, the cost advantage of a new machine or process might have been partially nullified. In any event, the job-protective policies of the skilled workers' unions were a frequent cause of strife, and as such might well have provided another deterrent to the installation of a new device, and hence another obstacle to technical progress. As to trade union wages policy, it has often been argued that a policy of holding the line, of refusing to accept any diminution in the 'standard rate', forces employers to keep abreast of the best practices and helps drive to the wall those employers who rest content with a mechanically imperfect or otherwise backward plant. Yet the case of ring-spinning in Lancashire (cited by the Webbs as an admirable instance of how a trade union faced with a skill-displacing innovation held the line by refusing to accept any diminution in the 'standard rate' [76]) shows that a 'hold-the-line' approach to wages might not *always* have hastened the spread of innovation. The ring-frame could make use of labour of a lesser order of skill than that required by the mule. When confronted with the demands of mule-using employers that mule-spinners accept lower piece-rates in order to compete with ring-frame mills employing unskilled women, the Amalgamated Association of Operative Cotton-spinners adopted the policy of permitting no 'lowering of the dyke' [77].

What [the employer] was offered was . . . a revision of the piece-work list so arranged as to stimulate him to augment the rapidity and complexity of the mule, in order that the mule-spinners increasing in dexterity, might simultaneously enlarge the output per machine and raise their own earnings. The cotton spinners in short . . . preferred to meet the competition of a new process by raising their own level of skill, rather than by degrading their Standard of Life. [78]

But was the consequence of this policy altogether desirable, if a rapid rate of technological advance is regarded as important? According to the Webbs, 'The result has been that, except under certain circumstances, the mule has, up to now [c. 1897], fairly held its own.' [79] (Still, it is quite likely that the relatively slow spread of ring-spinning in Britain was due rather more to the conservatism of the employers than to the stubbornness of the unions.) The author of 'The Crisis in British Industry' singled out the Sheffield scissors trade as a glaring example of how trade union intransigence on the wages question made it impossible for manufacturers to reap the full benefits of a new mechanical device – the scissors-stamping machine, in this instance. When British employers attempted

> to introduce stamping into the Sheffield trade, in place of forging, the grinders' union refused to make any concessions in price on having placed in their hands an article they could finish with less trouble than before. Consequently the Sheffield manufacturer found there would not be sufficient saving to justify his putting down stamping machinery, and he has had to be content to see the trade drift more and more into the hands of the Germans. [80]

He added that 'almost the same remarks apply to . . . razors', since a union's refusal to make piece-rates concessions in that trade prevented the installation of a mechanical process.

Is any of the evidence entirely conclusive, or must the question of the role of the trade union movement, and of the labour force generally, in Britain's industrial development remain by and large unresolved? Britain had the world's strongest trade union movement from the point of view of both density and sophistication of organization. Would this fact in itself have made the British industrial milieu rather less receptive to innovation than that of either the United States or Germany? Elie Halévy, in his monumental *History of the English People*, wrote that 'it was not surprising that the United States and Germany were outstripping England in the race for industrial supremacy. Neither Carnegie nor Krupp had to deal with trade unions' [81]. However, this statement is not wholly accurate. In the first place, Carnegie was not quite so fortunate. Even during the decades before the advent of the United Steel Workers of America, the steel industry of that country was not entirely bereft of unions (although, admittedly, the American steel industry of the early decades of the twentieth century must have appeared to the British iron and steel employers of that era, and to present-day American employers in the industry, as a kind of union-less valhalla). In the second place, and much more important, the tangle of determining circumstances is surely too complex to permit of the simple cause–effect relationship postulated by Halévy. The part played by labour in any well-reasoned explanation of retardation in British industry has to vie, for primacy of place, with a host of other factors – social and economic.

Still, trade union policies designed to preserve the sphere of the skilled operative could scarcely be said to have quickened the pace of technological advance in Britain. Moreover, conservatism in Britain knew no class lines, and there is some justification for the belief that Britain's working classes formed (and continue to form) the most conservative stratum of an essentially conservative society. In 1910, an article by a professional engineer on 'Roughing Tools for Lathe Work' appeared in the *English Mechanic and World of Science*. It is a fine example of a cautious, conservative reaction to innovation and, also, of that characteristically British preference for 'practical experience' rather than science. On trial in this instance was experimentation by feed and speed men with the cutting angles of machine-shop cutting tools. Pitted against such experimentation was the decidedly unscientific 'practical experience' of the man at the bench. In the eyes of the author, the latter won hands down, for scientific experimentation is costly, so the author alleged, and in this particular case merely confirmed facts that the old-style craftsman knew 'by a kind of intuition born of long experience' [82]. '[An efficient machine tool] is still dependent more on the workman's experience than the theoretical methods of the feed and speed man.' [83] Surely, most trade unionists could scarcely have agreed more. 'W.H.C.', who quoted the article *in extenso* in the Amalgamated Engineers' *Monthly Journal* for October 1910, is uncompromising in his approbation. 'The result of years of practical working is still the best base of observations.' [84] Then, for good measure, W.H.C. added that 'the speed and feed man is a useless non-producer, a nuisance who doesn't pay his way' [85]. 'Useless non-producer' strikes a distressingly familiar note – but a note scarcely confined to trade union circles.

APPENDICES TO CHAPTER 5

A

Further Case Studies in Working-Class and Official Trade Union Attitudes to Innovation

1 Further case studies in working-class and official trade union attitudes to innovation are provided by the reactions of workers and unions to the feed and speed system, the premium bonus wage incentive system, and technical education. (In fairness, it should be added that the first two of these were subject to considerable abuse by employers.) The feed and speed system, as already noted, was a supervisory device for increasing productivity. Its appearance in the engineering trades late in the nineteenth century provoked considerable hostility among workers placed under it, and trade union

leaders were outspoken in their denunciations. More than one scathing editorial on feed and speed is to be found in the ASE's *Monthly Journals* and *Reports* [1]. At the 1907 Trades Union Congress, a representative of the Tin and Iron Plate Workers introduced a resolution asking trade unions 'to use every effort to stop the further development [of the feed and speed system] and to take steps to abolish it wherever it has been introduced' [2]. The resolution (which was also directed against premium bonus) was carried 'by a large majority'. At the 1910 Congress, the Labour Protection League introduced a resolution for the abandonment of the feed and speed system 'in our national factories' [3].

The grounds for labour's hostility, reasonable or not, were at least understandable. In the first place, the feed and speed system introduced an additional element of overseership into the shop. Moreover, it was a kind of overseership that was apt to be viewed as a driving device by all workers [4], and as an affront to craft pride and individualism by the more tradition-minded of skilled operatives [5]. To many, it was a threat to more than mere craft pride: it was a threat to the existence of the craft itself, for it was sometimes regarded as yet another one of those devices that lowered skill requirements. After all, under the feed and speed system, appropriate speeds, feeds, and cutting angles were worked out, not by the machine-tool operator, but by a new kind of specialist [6]. And, of course, since feed and speed was a speeding-up device, it was bound to rub against the old fear of unemployment harboured by those still under the influence of the 'lump o' labour' belief. Thus, its supposed effect on employment was one of the grounds urged against it by the trade unionist who introduced the condemnatory resolution at the 1907 Trades Union Congress. Finally, where it was used to aid in the determination of piece-rates, the cry occasionally went up that one of its purposes was to depress both piece prices and earnings levels [7]. For all these reasons, therefore, feed and speed was thought to be subversive of the working man's best interests [8], and, in the words of the resolution presented to the 1907 TUC, 'utterly opposed to the principles of Trade Unionism' [9].

2   The premium bonus system, which was also gaining ground among employers during the early years of the present century, especially in the engineering trades, was another managerial device that caused considerable friction. A wage incentive scheme that

offered a bonus to the worker who completed a job in less than the 'standard time' allowed, it was resented by trade unionists as another of those speeding-up devices that were allegedly so destructive of the principles of trade unionism. Nevertheless, in spite of this hostility, no less a union than the Amalgamated Society of Engineers made its peace with the devil. In a covenant with the employers – the so-called 'Carlisle Agreement' of 1902 – the ASE undertook to accept the premium bonus plan in return for a number of safeguards. The safeguarding provisions guaranteed the current time rates of pay as minima, provided for overtime pay, forbade the reduction of basis times or prices once these had been fixed (except where a change in process necessitated some adjustment – an exception which provided much sustenance for the technical progress–worker 'obstructionism' debate), and forbade 'experimentation' to gauge the worker's capacity if the object was a return to day work [10]. Although the agreement was signed by the ASE's Executive Committee, it was never submitted to the membership for ratification [11]. The union's Organizing District Delegates were constantly reporting instances of members either refusing to work under premium bonus or protesting the methods adopted for setting basis times [12].

In 1909 the Trades Union Congress stepped into the fray and appointed a committee to inquire into the working of premium bonus. The committee reported in 1910 [13], and its report was, for the most part, one long condemnation.

Almost without exception the Premium Bonus system is condemned by all who have had practical experience of its working. It is urged against it –

[1] That it Destroys the Principle of Collective *Bargaining*. The workman has rarely any voice in the fixing of time allowances, and . . . although certain regulations and restrictions were imposed by the Carlisle Agreement, these safeguards are being continually and persistently evaded by employers . . .

[2] *That it is Destructive of Trade-unionism and Encourages Disorganisation* . . . almost without exception the whole of the trade unions representing [the engineering] industry show a considerable falling off in their membership. This may be due to many circumstances, but one of the chief factors in this falling off is undoubtedly the introduction and growth of the Premium Bonus System, which (a) is abolishing craftmanship by training vast numbers of specialists . . . (b) casualises labour, and so reduces the standard of living, making it impossible for many . . . to pay the heavy contributions required by . . . trade unions . . .

[3] *That it is one of the Causes of Unemployment* . . . [It] causes an all-round speeding-up. Time limits are being continually reduced . . .

[4] *The Premium Bonus System leads to Scamping of Work.*

[5] *That it Prevents the Proper Training of Apprentices.* Before the introduction of the Premium Bonus System lads were apprenticed to their trade, and their employers undertook to give them an all-round training. [But under premium bonus] they are kept to one special job . . .

[6] *The Premium Bonus System Promotes Selfishness in the Workshop.* Upon this point the witnesses were unanimous.

[7] *It Promotes Workshop Favouritism* . . .

The Committee concur in the whole of these conclusions. [14]

A vote among the unions involved with the system showed a ten to one majority in favour of abolition. Yet the ASE continued to accede, at least officially, to the Carlisle Agreement until 1914. In the meantime, there was constant strife between ASE branches and employers over the working of premium bonus, and several editorials and articles appeared in the union's *Monthly Journal* in condemnation of the system [15].

The trade union view of the matter was no doubt rather extreme, yet the business of having to fix 'standard times' under the premium bonus system provided a not unreasonable cause for concern, at least on some occasions. Therefore, as in the case of feed and speed, opposition to premium bonus did not spring solely from a preternatural conservatism or hostility to innovation *per se*, but from a certain amount of experience of either inept methods of basis-time fixing or actual malpractice [16]. Still, in so far as premium bonus brought productivity advantages – this would be extremely difficult to demonstrate empirically – it could be argued that here was yet another instance of trade unions standing in the way of 'progress'. But it cannot be conceded that those who so argue have an irrefutable case.

3   With technical education, we confront a different phenomenon and a different kind of reaction. The question of the adequacy or inadequacy of British technical education has already been raised. Whether or not the allegations of employer neglect and indifference can be substantiated, and the actual state of the facilities available for technical education aside, it is a fact that one could encounter blind prejudice to formal technical education, and to the lads turned out by technical schools, on the part of many old-style craftsmen. 'Of course I do not want to speak against technical education, but we find that

from technical schools and from the boys' institutes and those place
there is a preponderance of lads drafted into our trade more than into
any other.' This was a member of the ASE, expressing himself for the
benefit of the Labour Commission [17]. 'Of course I do not want to
speak against . . . *but* . . .': the qualifying clause speaks volumes. Was
this another case of trade union obstructiveness lying athwart the path
of progress, or was it merely one more example of how the appearance
of something new within the industrial *status quo* was apt to breed,
among all classes of the country, caution, hesitancy, and suspicion?

B
An Analysis of Labour Disputes, 1900–13

Those who fasten upon the antics of the trade union movement as
the explanation for any technical backwardness that major British
industries may have displayed would probably argue that the use
of the strike weapon was just as hurtful to technical progress as
quiet indulgence in restrictive practices. Many supporters of this
point of view would doubtless bring *all* strikes, regardless of cause,
within the purview of this observation. Others, more cautious,
might merely allege that only those strikes that originated in an
employer's attempt to introduce some new technique or method of
manufacture, or to employ a new class of labour, or to install a new
system of managing, deploying, or paying the labour force, or to
revise piece-rates consequent upon some technical or other change,
actually stood in the way of progress. If this point be conceded, then
the question arises, how large did this type of dispute loom in the
history of the industrial relations of the period? Statistical investigation might leave the question unresolved, since the data available
leave considerable room for 'interpretation'. It is possible, however,
with the aid of the Labour Department's Annual Reports on Strikes
and Lock-outs, to get at least some notion of the relative importance
of this type of dispute. Tables 8 and 9 show the relative importance,
as indicated by the numbers directly involved, of disputes having to do
with the introduction (or attempted introduction) of a new system of
wage payment (or a revision of existing rates following a change in work
methods or conditions), the employment of a new class of labour,
or some unspecified change in working arrangements and conditions.

From Table 8 it may be seen that in British industry as a whole,
during the entire period 1900–13, disputes in the above-mentioned

TABLE 8

Analysis of Disputes, United Kingdom, 1900-13. All Trades

Principal cause of dispute	1900		1901	
	Number of workpeople directly involved	Number of workpeople directly involved as a % of total no. directly involved in all disputes	Number of workpeople directly involved	Number of workpeople directly involved as a % of total no. directly involved in all disputes
1 System of payment of wages	1,987	1·5	5,440	4·9
2 Readjustment of rates of payment because of change in working conditions	1,576	1·2	5,414	4·9
3 Employment of labourers instead of skilled workmen	1,300	1·0	316	0·3
4 Employment of women instead of men	34	—	90	0·1
5 Employment of apprentices and boys	586	0·4	358	0·3
6 Working arrangements, rules, etc.	18,956	14·0	23,185	20·8
Total directly involved in above types of dispute	24,439	18·1	34,803	31·3
Total, all disputes	135,145	100·0	111,437	100·0

Principal cause of dispute	1902		1903	
	Number of workpeople directly involved	Number of workpeople directly involved as a % of total no. directly involved in all disputes	Number of workpeople directly involved	Number of workpeople directly involved as a % of total no. directly involved in all disputes
1 System of payment of wages	618	0·5	14,914	15·9
2 Readjustment of rates of payment because of change in working conditions	10,009	8·6	6,397	6·8
3 Employment of labourers instead of skilled workmen	248	0·2	186	0·2
4 Employment of women instead of men	187	0·2	25	—
5 Employment of apprentices and boys	286	0·2	106	0·1
6 Working arrangements, rules, etc.	19,849	17·0	13,609	14·6
Total directly involved in above types of dispute	31,197	26·7	35,237	37·6
Total, all disputes	116,824	100·0	93,515	100·0

TABLE 8 (*continued*)

Principal cause of dispute	1904		1905	
	Number of workpeople directly involved	Number of workpeople directly involved as a % of total no. directly involved in all disputes	Number of workpeople directly involved	Number of workpeople directly involved as a % of total no. directly involved in all disputes
1 System of payment of wages	669	1·2	645	1·0
2 Readjustment of rates of payment because of change in working conditions	11,752	21·0	10,149	15·0
3 Employment of labourers instead of skilled workmen	180	0·3	73	0·1
4 Employment of women instead of men	106	0·2	61	0·1
5 Employment of apprentices and boys	566	1·0	397	0·6
6 Working arrangements, rules, etc.	7,601	13·6	5,546	8·2
Total directly involved in above types of dispute	20,874	37·3	16,871	25·0
Total, all disputes	56,060	100·0	67,653	100·0

Principal cause of dispute	1906		1907	
	Number of workpeople directly involved	Number of workpeople directly involved as a % of total no. directly involved in all disputes	Number of workpeople directly involved	Number of workpeople directly involved as a % of total no. directly involved in all disputes
1 System of payment of wages	821	0·5	3,095	3·1
2 Readjustment of rates of payment because of change in working conditions	6,713	4·3	22,461	22·3
3 Employment of labourers instead of skilled workmen	800	0·5	409	0·4
4 Employment of women instead of men	10	—	154	0·2
5 Employment of apprentices and boys	235	0·1	4,811	4·8
6 Working arrangements, rules, etc.	6,536	4·1	11,802	11·7
Total directly involved in above types of dispute	15,115	9·5	42,732	42·5
Total, all disputes	157,872	100·0	100,728	100·0

TABLE 8 (*continued*)

Principal cause of dispute	1908		1909	
	Number of workpeople directly involved	Number of workpeople directly involved as a % of total no. directly involved in all disputes	Number of workpeople directly involved	Number of workpeople directly involved as a % of total no. directly involved in all disputes
1 System of payment of wages	1,787	0·8	2,219	1·3
2 Readjustment of rates of payment because of change in working conditions	4,335	1·9	2,734	1·6
3 Employment of labourers instead of skilled workmen	42	—	1,078	0·6
4 Employment of women instead of men	197	0·1	41	—
5 Employment of apprentices and boys	40	—	133	0·1
6 Working arrangements, rules, etc.	12,467	5·6	8,892	5·2
Total directly involved in above types of dispute	18,868	8·4	15,097	8·8
Total, all disputes	223,967	100·0	170,250	100·0

Principal cause of dispute	1910		1911	
	Number of workpeople directly involved	Number of workpeople directly involved as a % of total no. directly involved in all disputes	Number of workpeople directly involved	Number of workpeople directly involved as a % of total no. directly involved in all disputes
1 System of payment of wages	3,621	0·9	4,365	0·5
2 Readjustment of rates of payment because of change in working conditions	40,503	10·5	14,855	1·8
3 Employment of labourers instead of skilled workmen	110	—	1,066	0·1
4 Employment of women instead of men	14	—	109	—
5 Employment of apprentices and boys	346	0·1	65	—
6 Working arrangements, rules, etc.	62,207	16·2	68,009	8·2
Total directly involved in above types of dispute	106,801	27·2	88,469	10·6
Total, all disputes	385,085	100·0	831,104	100·0

TABLE 3 (continued)

Principal cause of dispute	1912		1913	
	Number of workpeople directly involved	Number of workpeople directly involved as a % of total no. directly involved in all disputes	Number of workpeople directly involved	Number of workpeople directly involved as a % of total no. directly involved in all disputes
1 System of payment of wages	892	0·1	4,320	0·8
2 Readjustment of rates of payment because of change in working conditions	18,102	1·5	12,910	2·5
3 Employment of labourers instead of skilled workmen	1,267	0·1	1,773	0·3
4 Employment of women instead of men	10	—	884	0·2
5 Employment of apprentices and boys	331	—	882	0·2
6 Working arrangements, rules, etc.	42,068	3·4	20,159	3·9
Total directly involved in above types of dispute	62,670	5·1	40,928	7·9
Total, all disputes	1,233,016	100·0	516,037	100·0

Principal cause of dispute	1900 to 1913, inclusive	
1 System of payment of wages	45,393	1·1
2 Readjustment of rates of payment because of change in working conditions	167,910	4·0
3 Employment of labourers instead of skilled workmen	8,848	0·2
4 Employment of women instead of men	1,922	—
5 Employment of apprentices and boys	9,142	0·2
6 Working arrangements, rules, etc.	320,886	7·6
Total directly involved in above types of dispute	554,101	13·1
Total, all disputes	4,198,693	100·0

SOURCE: Board of Trade (Labour Dept.), Annual Reports on Strikes and Lock-outs in the UK.

TABLE 9

Analysis of Disputes, United Kingdom, 1900-13. Metal, Engineering, and Shipbuilding Trades.

Principal cause of dispute	1900		1901	
	Number of workpeople directly involved	Number of workpeople directly involved as a % of total no. directly involved in all disputes in the group	Number of workpeople directly involved	Number of workpeople directly involved as a % of total no. directly involved in all disputes in the group
1 System of payment of wages	887	8·5	653	4·8
2 Readjustment of rates of payment because of change in working conditions	168	1·6	1,283	9·4
3 Employment of labourers instead of skilled workmen	184	1·8	263	1·9
4 Employment of women instead of men	—	—	—	—
5 Employment of apprentices and boys	470	4·5	347	2·5
6 Working arrangements, rules, etc.	757	7·3	4,663	34·0
Total directly involved in above types of dispute	2,466	23·7	7,209	52·6
Total, metal, engineering, and shipbuilding group	10,400	100·0	13,720	100·0

Principal cause of dispute	1902		1903	
	Number of workpeople directly involved	Number of workpeople directly involved as a % of total no. directly involved in all disputes in the group	Number of workpeople directly involved	Number of workpeople directly involved as a % of total no. directly involved in all disputes in the group
1 System of payment of wages	162	1·7	14,181	51·1
2 Readjustment of rates of payment because of change in working conditions	128	1·3	399	1·4
3 Employment of labourers instead of skilled workmen	196	2·0	149	0·5
4 Employment of women instead of men	—	—	—	—
5 Employment of apprentices and boys	230	2·4	74	0·3
6 Working arrangements, rules, etc.	1,604	16·7	2,575	9·3
Total directly involved in above types of dispute	2,320	24·1	17,378	62·6
Total, metal, engineering, and shipbuilding group	9,630	100·0	27,756	100·0

TABLE 9 (continued)

Principal cause of dispute	1904		1905	
	Number of workpeople directly involved	Number of workpeople directly involved as a % of total no. directly involved in all disputes in the group	Number of workpeople directly involved	Number of workpeople directly involved as a % of total no. directly involved in all disputes in the group
1 System of payment of wages	125	1·4	59	0·8
2 Readjustment of rates of payment because of change in working conditions	385	4·5	486	6·5
3 Employment of labourers instead of skilled workmen	180	2·1	53	0·7
4 Employment of women instead of men	31	0·4	—	—
5 Employment of apprentices and boys	500	5·8	397	5·3
6 Working arrangements, rules, etc.	662	7·7	840	11·3
Total directly involved in above types of dispute	1,883	21·9	1,835	24·6
Total, metal, engineering, and shipbuilding group	8,649	100·0	7,458	100·0

Principal cause of dispute	1906		1907	
1 System of payment of wages	120	0·5	1,513	12·7
2 Readjustment of rates of payment because of change in working conditions	345	1·5	477	4·0
3 Employment of labourers instead of skilled workmen	800	3·4	391	3·3
4 Employment of women instead of men	—	—	—	—
5 Employment of apprentices and boys	129	0·6	102	0·9
6 Working arrangements, rules, etc.	1,448	6·2	429	3·6
Total directly involved in above types of dispute	2,842	12·2	2,912	24·5
Total, metal, engineering, and shipbuilding group	23,389	100·0	11,898	100·0

TABLE 9 (*continued*)

Principal cause of dispute	1908 — Number of workpeople directly involved	1908 — Number of workpeople directly involved as a % of total no. directly involved in all disputes in the group	1909 — Number of workpeople directly involved	1909 — Number of workpeople directly involved as a % of total no. directly involved in all disputes in the group
1 System of payment of wages	27	0·1	572	8·8
2 Readjustment of rates of payment because of change in working conditions	92	0·3	681	10·4
3 Employment of labourers instead of skilled workmen	42	0·1	233	3·6
4 Employment of women instead of men	—	—	—	—
5 Employment of apprentices and boys	—	—	42	0·6
6 Working arrangements, rules, etc.	904	3·1	511	7·8
Total directly involved in above types of dispute	1,065	3·6	2,039	31·2
Total, metal, engineering, and shipbuilding group	29,020	100·0	6,518	100·0

Principal cause of dispute	1910 — Number of workpeople directly involved	1910 — Number of workpeople directly involved as a % of total no. directly involved in all disputes in the group	1911 — Number of workpeople directly involved	1911 — Number of workpeople directly involved as a % of total no. directly involved in all disputes in the group
1 System of payment of wages	818	2·7	1,629	2·2
2 Readjustment of rates of payment because of change in working conditions	1,695	5·5	1,466	2·0
3 Employment of labourers instead of skilled workmen	97	0·3	1,054	1·4
4 Employment of women instead of men	—	—	34	0·1
5 Employment of apprentices and boys	—	—	55	
6 Working arrangements, rules, etc.	18,160	59·4	2,704	3·7
Total directly involved in above types of dispute	20,770	67·9	6,942	9·4
Total, metal, engineering, and shipbuilding group	30,575	100·0	74,004	100·0

TABLE 7 (continued)

Principal cause of dispute	1912		1913	
	Number of workpeople directly involved	Number of workpeople directly involved as a % of total no. directly involved in all disputes in the group	Number of workpeople directly involved	Number of workpeople directly involved as a % of total no. directly involved in all disputes in the group
1 System of payment of wages	418	0·6	2,447	2·4
2 Readjustment of rates of payment because of change in working conditions	1,854	2·8	1,138	1·1
3 Employment of labourers instead of skilled workmen	975	1·5	1,759	1·7
4 Employment of women instead of men	10	—	10	—
5 Employment of apprentices and boys	260	0·4	613	0·6
6 Working arrangements, rules, etc.	4,643	7·0	3,980	3·9
Total directly involved in above types of dispute	8,160	12·3	9,947	9·7
Total, metal, engineering, and shipbuilding group	66,500	100·0	102,251	100·0

Principal cause of dispute	1900–13, inclusive	
1 System of payment of wages	23,611	5·6
2 Readjustment of rates of payment because of change in working conditions	10,597	2·5
3 Employment of labourers instead of skilled workmen	6,376	1·5
4 Employment of women instead of men	85	—
5 Employment of apprentices and boys	3,219	0·8
6 Working arrangements, rules, etc.	43,880	10·4
Total directly involved in above types of dispute	87,768	20·8
Total, metal, engineering, and shipbuilding group	421,768	100·0

SOURCE: Board of Trade (Labour Dept.), Annual Reports on Strikes and Lock-outs in the UK.

categories never accounted, in any one year, for more than thirty-eight per cent of all workers who went on strike. Aggregating the data (in Table 8) for all fourteen years, it will be seen that these disputes accounted for about thirteen per cent of all workers who went on strike during the period. Turning to the metal, engineering, and shipbuilding group (Table 9), we find the percentages (of total numbers on strike in the group) accounted for by those involved in 'innovation' disputes rather higher than the percentages for industry as a whole, as would be expected in view of the part played by innovation in the industries in question. The group high for any one year was sixty-eight per cent (1904). The aggregate percentage for the group for the entire fourteen-year period was slightly under twenty-one per cent.

For both industry as a whole, and the metal, engineering, and shipbuilding group, the most prominent category of dispute – again, as indicated by the numbers of workers directly involved – among the six categories listed in the Tables was that relating to disputes over 'working arrangements, rules, etc'. For British industry as a whole, such disputes accounted for over seven-and-a-half per cent of the total number who went on strike during the 1900–13 period, while for the metal, engineering, and shipbuilding group, these disputes accounted for roughly ten-and-a-half per cent of all those employees in the group who went on strike during this period. Second in importance, in the case of industry as a whole, were disputes arising out of readjustments or attempted readjustments in rates of pay following a change in working conditions; while for the metal, engineering, and shipbuilding group, second place went to disputes over the method of wage payment – vivid testimony to the strife provoked by the introduction of the premium bonus system and similar systems of payment by results in these trades [1].

Does anything conclusive emerge from Tables 8 and 9? The data do not seem to lend much support to those who adopt an unreservedly anti-union or anti-labour position in the debate over industrial efficiency. Even if we grant that attempts to innovate within the realms of technology and organization did spawn a host of disputes, does this lend substantial support to the belief that the *major* share of blame for alleged technical or organizational backwardness must be laid at the door of labour? Strikes, together with restrictive practices, must be weighed in the balance with a variety of other possible causes of retardation.

110

The Economics of Retardation

What support is there for the belief that technical and organizational backwardness in British industry also had its more narrowly economic causes? This important aspect of the retardation story is far from clear. Possible economic roots of the alleged British failure to remain abreast of the most advanced industrial techniques are many and varied. The more widely discussed economic factors have included the economic consequences of the supposed inferiority of Britain's natural resource endowment; the size of the British manufacturing economy and of the key industries within that economy; the size and character of the demand and markets for British goods; disadvantages arising from techniques of business organization and industrial financing; the alleged handicap of Britain's early start as an industrial power and the alleged deterrent effect of existing plant and previous large-scale investment; the economic consequences of demographic trends; the appearance of international disparities, adverse to Britain, in the rates of increase of national product, including the export component of that product; problems arising out of the 'mix' of the British export bill; the export of capital from Britain; the influence of non- and anti-competitive behaviour in British industry; and, finally, free trade.

The Resource Base

In Chapter 1 quantitative and qualitative differences in the natural resource base were examined as possible explanations of productivity differences, the relationship being assumed to be a direct one. It is also possible for the resource base to affect productivity *indirectly* through its influence upon the choice of industrial techniques. To what extent, then, was Britain's relatively inferior resource endowment responsible for the technical lag in British industry? Consider, for example, the matter of fuel and power resources. Britain had neither natural gas nor petroleum. Her potential for hydroelectric power development was infinitesimal compared to that of the United States. Even with respect to a fuel in which Britain was singularly well-endowed, coal, there were important qualitative differences which were reflected in higher real costs of extraction and utilization in Britain [1]. It could thus be argued that a relative shortage of hydro power, and the fact that higher coal costs might tell against Britain when it came to the production of thermal power, would act as a retardative factor with respect to electrification. As to gas, natural is cheaper, in real terms, than coal gas, and hence confers some advantage over the latter with respect to aggregate productivity ratios. Then, too, if coal gas was more expensive than natural gas, and if there was an immense disparity as regards petroleum resources, might not the consequence be a lag in the development of new and additional sources of motive power and in the development and installation of new types of prime movers, and, hence in the advance of mechanization itself? Britain's position as a world trader would not have entirely offset this particular chain of disadvantages. Hydro power and natural gas are not exportable.

Precisely how serious were Britain's fuel and power disadvantages? Britain was rich in coal. Qualitative disadvantages here were surely marginal in comparison, say, to indifferent entrepreneurship. Nor is dependence upon steam engines, or upon thermal power instead of hydro power – even if thermal power is more expensive than hydro power, or even if thermal power can be produced more cheaply elsewhere – to be accounted a retardative influence of overwhelming significance. As to the petroleum disadvantage, it was very materially reduced by Britain's trade ties. If Britain was slow to electrify, or slow to adopt the internal combustion engine and other transmuters of motive power, the answer must, to a very considerable extent, lie elsewhere than in the sources of energy available.

Related to the natural resource debate was the question of the importance of the frontier of settlement in the United States for technical and organizational progress in that country. The presence in the United States of a frontier of settlement and the resulting opportunities for both working people and owners of capital meant that there was a relative scarcity of both labour *and* capital. The commonly accepted account of the long-run changes that took place in factor use and factor price relationships in the United States is usually confined to the scarcity of labour and the consequent search for labour-saving techniques. But, as Professor Frankel and Mr W. Duane Evans have pointed out [2], the opportunities provided by the frontier were a cause of the relative shortage of *capital* as well as labour, and hence provided a spur to continuing efforts to devise techniques which would economize on the use of the capital factor too [3]. This was a spur that was of course absent in Britain.

The frontier of settlement in the United States also helped to mould American attitudes to enterprise and innovation. Life on the frontier bred restlessness, ingenuity, and individualism – qualities that favoured the exercise of initiative and a high level of receptiveness to innovation. This is the familiar Turner thesis [4]. It has since been modified considerably. But in whatever particular it has been questioned, there is no doubt that there existed in the shifting frontier of settlement in the United States at least one beneficial influence on attitudes to industrial change that did not exist in the United Kingdom.

Size of Manufacturing Economy

A popular notion has it that the tremendous size of the American manufacturing economy, and of the individual industries within that economy, played an important part in conferring upon American manufacturing industry a high level of efficiency. But how closely has industrial size ever correlated with industrial efficiency? And was the size of the British manufacturing economy, and of the industries within that economy, so much smaller than the American as to belong to entirely different orders of magnitude?

Efforts to correlate size of industry and efficiency have yielded little that is conclusive. Certainly the studies of Rostas [5] and Frankel [6] of Anglo-American productivity differences, and the magnitudes of the coefficients of correlation that they computed for industrial size and industrial efficiency, lend scant support to the notion that size is of paramount importance for efficiency. Possibly all that the available evidence entitles us to say is that there *might* be *some* relationship between size and efficiency, but that most probably this relationship is weaker than what a good deal of the *a priori* thinking on the matter would have us believe [7]. On the other hand, magnitudes of correlation coefficients aside, it is a fact that the large manufacturing economy and the large industry afford greater opportunities for specialization than do smaller manufacturing economies and smaller industries. Moreover, in the very large manufacturing economy, the presence of industrial giants need not be as destructive of competitive behaviour and of the efficiency that such behaviour allegedly breeds as they would be in a smaller economy [8].

The critical point, however, is whether the British manufacturing economy, and major British manufacturing industries, were so very small relative to the American manufacturing economy and American industries of six and seven decades ago. It can scarcely be said that the British manufacturing economy was completely dwarfed by the American, either from the point of view of numbers employed or gross value of output, although, admittedly, the disparity as regards

TABLE 10

Numbers Employed in Manufacturing Industry, United Kingdom and United States, 1877–1910

Year	United Kingdom[a] Employment in thousands	Year	United States Employment in thousands
1877–85	4,750	1880	3,210
1886–93	5,160	1890	4,620
1894–1903	5,460	1900	6,250 (old series) / 6,090 (new series)
1904–10	5,660	1910	8,990

[a] The British figures relate to an interval rather than a single year, the midpoints of the intervals being used as benchmarks.

SOURCE: Frankel, *British and American Manufacturing Productivity*, p 84.

TABLE 11

Gross Value of Outputs, Manufacturing Industry, United Kingdom and United States, 1905 and 1907

Year	United Kingdom ($ millions)	United States ($ millions)
1905	—	14,802
1907	6,887	—

SOURCES: United Kingdom: Computed from B. R. Mitchell, *Abstract of British Historical Statistics* (Cambridge, Cambridge University Press, 1962), p 270.

United States: US Bureau of the Census, *Manufactures 1905*, Part I, p xxxv.

the latter was not entirely insignificant. (See Tables 10 and 11.) At any rate, the British manufacturing economy was not so small as to inhibit the spread of specialization or to make growth in the size of firm *necessarily* destructive of competition in every industry. Admittedly, there may have been less vigorous competitive behaviour in various British industries as compared to these same industries in the United States [9], but this had nothing to do with size of industry or manufacturing economy. On balance, then, neither size of manufacturing economy nor size of individual industries are to be accounted retardative influences in the British case.

Size of Market, Nature of Demand, and the Mass Production Technique

Britain's relative backwardness with respect to the mass production technique has often been attributed to factors having to do with the size of the market for the products of Britain's industries, with the nature of the demand for these products, or with both of these. As to the first, it is to be borne in mind that the choice of intra-plant techniques is in part a function of the constraints imposed by plant size, and plant size is in turn determined, in part at least (according to a familiar line of reasoning), by market size. This being so, did the sheer size of the American market confer yet another advantage upon that country's industries?

The market for the products of Britain's industries, although not coterminous with the boundaries of a single, large continental area, as in the case of the United States, nevertheless could scarcely be considered a *small* one. It was world-wide in scope, and, more importantly, it embraced large numbers of human beings. Even the British domestic market embraced a relatively large population. (In 1871, the British population was not so very much smaller than the American [10].) Furthermore, Britain's island position adjacent to the large populations of Western Europe meant that British manufacturers could gain access to other important markets (albeit diminished by tariff barriers) at transport costs well below those incurred by manufacturers of the eastern United States who were probing the western hinterland [11]. Using a more apt measure of market size, national income (Table 12), we can see that in 1870 the British domestic market was of an order of magnitude comparable to the American.

TABLE 12

National Income, United Kingdom and United States, 1869–1910

Year	United Kingdom ($ millions)	Year	United States[a] ($ millions)
1870	4,500	1869–73	6,200
1880	5,200	1877–81	8,500
1890	6,700	1887–91	11,000
1900	8,500	1900	14,600
1910	9,600	1910	27,200

[a] The US estimates for 1869–91 are five-year averages, and are for net national product instead of national income.

SOURCES: United Kingdom: Computed from B.R. Mitchell, *op. cit.*, pp 367–8.

United States: US Bureau of the Census, *Historical Statistics of the United States, Colonial Times to 1957* (Washington, DC, Government Printing Office, 1960), p 139.

However, the important point is that at a time when the British and American *domestic* markets were still roughly comparable in size, that is, during the early eighteen-seventies, American superiority as regards various elements of the mass production technique was *already* discernible. Indeed, some students of comparative industrial efficiency have pointed out that this superiority can be traced back to at least the eighteen-sixties if not earlier. In 1854, the commission sent by the British Ordnance Department to study American methods of small arms manufacture was most favourably impressed by the extent to which standardization and the techniques of large-scale repetition production had been applied to the manufacture of small arms, clocks, and various hardware items [12].

Moreover, is it always the case that specialization, standardization, continuous flow production, and the other components of the mass production technique can only be practised where the giant market holds sway? Rostas's Anglo-American productivity comparisons are illuminating on this point (even though they relate to the nineteen-thirties and nineteen-forties rather than to the period under consideration).

[We] find that the market for US industry . . . is in most cases greater in the US than in the UK. It is about equal in wool and margarine and smaller in bricks and fish curing. In such industries as iron and steel, machinery,

116

motor cars, rubber tyres, electric bulbs, tin cans, glass containers, wireless sets, matches and ice, the US market is appreciably greater than the British market. There is some inter-relationship between size of the market and productivity in the sense that the greatest relative advantage in productivity in the US is shown in industries where the US market is relatively very big (tin cans, rubber tyres, motor cars, wireless sets, electric lamps, matches). In one case (fish curing), a smaller US market goes with smaller productivity. But otherwise there does not appear to be a close inter-relationship. In cases where the US market is big (e.g. steel), relative productivity advantage is not above average. The same is true in such cases as ice, though this is a strongly localized industry with hosts of small plants, which may explain why the US advance in productivity is below average. There is no sign of inter-relationship between productivity and size of market in other cases either. In soap or biscuits, for example, US productivity is relatively high, though the size of the industry is not appreciably greater than in the UK. Also in a number of industries where the size of the industry is the same or smaller than in Britain (e.g. breweries, wool) there is an advance in productivity in the US.

While it is obvious from this comparison that in certain industries the size of the market has an influence on output per worker, this is not as great as is usually assumed. If we compare the relative productivity and the size of the market in UK industry in relation to Sweden and Holland, we can see that relative productivity is in no way related to the size of the market. This points to the fact that optimum plant (or firm) and specialization can be achieved within the limits of a smaller plant (output). [13]

And, presumably, it should be possible to implement various of the other facets of the mass production technique, including standardization, 'within the limits of a smaller market' – given, of course, the existence of optimum-size plant.

At the same time, market size should not be completely ruled out as a limiting factor as regards the mass production technique. After all, the optimum-size plant may require, typically, a relatively large market. But the essential point is that the British market was in fact relatively large – certainly large enough for the optimum-size plant and mass production techniques – and yet there was still a noticeable difference between Britain and the United States with respect to the extent of adoption of mass production techniques.

It has also been argued that differences in the *character* of the markets for British and American goods, or, more precisely, in the internal composition of the total demand for these goods, contributed, to some extent, to the observed differences in manufacturing technique.

Among the more zealous proponents of this demand argument are those who fasten primarily on Britain's dependence upon the varied demands of *external* markets. The argument runs along familiar lines. Britain's dependence upon external markets had, as one of its consequences, neglect of specialization, standardization, and all the other components of the mass production technique. This is to be contrasted with America's experience. During the last quarter of the nineteenth century, the market for America's manufactures was provided to an overwhelming extent by a rapidly growing American population. Dependence upon external demand was negligible. Moreover, with the continuing assimilation of an immigrant populace, the American domestic market came to be increasingly characterized by homogeneity of demand. And the relatively uniform demands of a vast continental market provided American manufacturers with an important precondition for a 'take-off' into a new era of large-scale production of relatively standardized goods. In the British case, on the other hand, external demand, far from diminishing in importance, came to be more of a lifeline than ever during the second half of the nineteenth century. Moreover, an external trade which was not only global in scope but which encompassed markets with radically differing requirements could scarcely have provided the most favourable setting for the mass production technique.

But this variant of the demand argument diminishes in strength as soon as one takes into account certain inter-industry differences in both products and processes. Such differences include those with respect to the variety of products that can be made with an industry's existing productive facilities, and, also, those with respect to the simplicity or complexity of products and processes. In export-oriented industries such as the cotton industry, the range of products is narrower, the products themselves are simpler in conception or design, and certainly most of the processes involved are simpler, than is the case with many of the products and processes of an exporting industry like engineering [14]. Surely the essential nature of an industry's products, and of the technics of production involved, have as much weight as determinants of degree of specialization and standardization, and of other facets of the mass production technique, as does mere dependence upon export markets [15].

In any event, if demand arguments are to be considered at all, the focus must be upon *total demand* and not merely the export component of that total, even if the export component does happen to loom large. Obviously the character of the total demand for a product will have some bearing on whether or not that product will be subjected to a high degree of standardization or will be produced in an enormous range of different styles, shapes, and sizes. As to consumer goods, as has already been intimated, it has often been argued that the social pressures of the American melting pot militated against highly individualistic consumer behaviour and conduced to a high degree of standardization of tastes. In Britain, on the other hand, negligible immigration into the country and relative ethnic homogeneity meant that the social pressures for uniformity of demand were never present to the same extent as they were in the United States. Add to this the fact that in Britain 'aristocratic' tastes extended beyond the aristocracy *per se* and that these tastes were not such as to conduce to uniformity, and the result is a market for consumer goods in which craftsmanship, individuality, and above all, variety, become important desiderata [16]. And of course if to the domestic demand for the products of British industry we add the various overseas demands, the market that emerges is one that was not as favourable to the methods of massive-scale, standardized production as was the American. Still, demand factors do not provide the whole explanation for British tardiness in adopting mass production techniques [17].

Problems of Business Organization and Finance

Were forms of business organization and financing arrangements for British manufacturing industry adequate to the task of financing such real capital formation as mass production techniques might require? The prerequisites here would include the corporate form with limited liability, ample pools of savings and well-developed long-term capital markets.

Although Britain had general provision for limited liability (1856 and 1862) before Germany, the principal industrial states of the United States had enacted general limited liability laws before either of the other two countries. Quite early on, therefore, corporate structures suitable to the eventual adoption of mass production techniques were legally permissive in the United States. But really how important for real capital formation and technological advance in manufacturing industry, during the eighteen-forties, 'fifties and 'sixties, was the joint stock form with limited liability? At least one member of the British industrial commissions that visited the United States in the early 'fifties thought it was. The corporation laws of that country were a tremendous boon to the further development of factory industry, he reported, and had already 'led to a much greater development of the industrial resources and skill of the country than ... could have resulted from mere private enterprise [that is, sole proprietorships and partnerships]' [18]. Still, British law did permit the joint stock form with limited liability, and this at least two or more decades prior to the *widespread* appearance, in any country, of those manufacturing techniques characteristic of the second industrial revolution. But during those same years, when there were no great legal barriers to adopting limited liability in Britain, limited liability and in some cases even the joint stock form itself were far from typical in British manufacturing industry. In fact, limited liability was not adopted very widely in Britain until the eighteen-eighties.

Moreover, when the privilege of limited liability became the law of the land in England, and for several years thereafter, many very large firms continued to operate as partnerships or sole proprietorships, and apparently without having to face acute problems of long-term financing. It seems doubtful, therefore, that the achievement of optimum scale or the spread of the mass production technique itself, in Britain, was inhibited by slowness to adopt the corporate form and limited liability.

Nor could it be said that the British economy was deficient as regards either the propensity to save or the provision of institutional means in the long-term capital market for marshalling savings. It has, however, occasionally been said that the relative absence of continental or American-type investment banks in Britain to some extent militated against the development of large-scale undertakings in that country. Investment banks had played roles of more or less prominence in financing industrial development in France, Germany, and the United States. Moreover, in Germany the investment banking function was not confined solely to investment banks *per se*, for many ordinary banks of deposit in that country catered to the long-term capital needs of industrial undertakings. In Britain, investment banking never became a significant phenomenon, although during the eighteen-sixties several investment finance companies of questionable stability were formed, ostensibly for the purpose of making long-term loans. Many of these houses went under in the panic of 1866. It is true that some of the merchant banks in Britain, for example, Barings and Rothschilds, also began to perform investment bank functions, but the ordinary commercial banks of the country remained what they had always been – primarily short-term lenders.

On the other hand, the more mature British economy possessed what her less mature rivals did not (or at least not to the same extent) – old industrial undertakings able to indulge in a very considerable measure of *self*-financing. Hence the relatively greater need in the United States and Germany for constant resort to the corporate form and the long-term capital market, and, also, to investment banking facilities. Possibly, more highly developed investment banking in Britain might have done something to encourage the entry into British industry of large numbers of adventurous, growth-minded newcomers. Still, in the absence of well-developed investment banking, newcomers with a penchant for daring could still take advantage of the corporate form from almost mid-century on, and, some of them, of equity markets which were second to none in the world, to help solve problems of capital formation. The relative neglect of investment banking in Britain is therefore not to be accounted a major retardative factor.

The 'Handicap of an Early Start'

One of the penalties, it is often argued, of being first to arrive at the various thresholds of a new industrial era is to become saddled, during those crucial years when other countries begin their advance to industrialization, with much of the plant and equipment of the early phases of industrial revolution. The newcomers are not so encumbered. They enjoy the fruits of a more recent technology. They will therefore have productivity advantages. And they will also have a national equipment which might prove more adaptable to current and future changes in technique and organization.

The validity of these arguments in the case of Britain, the United States, and Germany has not been uncontested. For one thing, the alleged earliness of Britain's early start can be diminished in magnitude by a more careful scrutiny of the record. Those who make much of the early start argument seldom bother to pinpoint in time those decades which saw manufacturing in the United States emerge from near-negligibility to a position of significance in the national economy. Indeed, the chronology of industrialization in Britain, the United States, and Germany eliminates some of the cogency of the early start argument. In the eighteen-eighties both Germany and the United States were already major manufacturing powers: even ten years earlier neither country could be considered insignificant as a manufacturer. In 1870, for example, when Britain's share of world manufacturing output was thirty-two per cent, that of the United States was twenty-three per cent and that of Germany thirteen per cent [19]. Thus, during the eighteen-eighties and 'nineties when important innovations in manufacturing technology were being introduced in the United States and Germany, in neither case were they being introduced into manufacturing economies that had only recently sprung into being. Britain, it is true, had had an earlier start, and was saddled with industrial equipment which was on the whole older than that of the two newer powers, but it is quite likely that this disadvantage was beginning to diminish in importance, at least relatively, during the period under consideration.

At any rate, the alleged orders of magnitude of the differences in equipment age as between Britain and the newer industrial countries have been called into question. The statistical difficulties here are of course immense. As far as recent decades are concerned it has been suggested that the differences in the ages of the capital equipment of Britain and the United States were not as great as might be imagined [20]. On the other hand, there are some grounds for believing that the disparities in equipment age as between Britain and the United States were greater during the several decades prior to the depression of the nineteen-thirties than they were during and after the depression. Terborgh's findings serve to strengthen this impression. According to Terborgh, in 1925 only forty-four per cent of machine tools in use in the United States were more than ten years old; in 1935 the proportion was sixty-five per cent, and in 1940 it was seventy per cent [21]. And the same tendency to prolong the average age of equipment is shown for locomotives and railroad freight cars in use in the United States during the nineteen-thirties. It might well have been, therefore, that some degree of difference in the ages of the equipment in use in the two countries obtained during the first decade of the present century and earlier, even if the difference was less than what preconceptions on the matter had led students to believe. Certainly, this is a supposition which is reconcilable with the proven condition of relative technical lag in British manufacturing industry at the time.

Moreover, do we have in this supposition not only a symptom but another partial explanation of Britain's relative lag? Older equipment usually does not lend itself so readily to the most advanced techniques of manufacturing, especially where these techniques have been evolved within the matrix of the latest equipment available and, in addition, involve continuous flow production. Then, too, there is also the possible disadvantage of becoming encumbered with outmoded ideas and a generally out-of-date approach to problems of technology and organization.

The Alleged Deterrent Effect of Existing Plant and Previous Large-Scale Investment

Granted a degree of disparity between the ages of the installed plant of the British and American economies, was it also the case, as has frequently been argued, that the existence of older plant in Britain constituted a colossal *financial* barrier in the way of re-equipment? In its simplest form the argument has usually centred upon the necessity to continue writing off huge sunk costs or upon the replacement costs involved, or upon both of these. For example, it has been alleged that during the last century the investment in existing facilities for the production of steam and gas in Britain militated against electrification. Ostensibly, the more capital-intensive an industry, the more compelling this reasoning becomes. Iron- and steel-making was the most capital-intensive of all industries, and some of those who advanced the 'existing plant' argument contended that in iron and steel the heavy capital outlays of an earlier generation, coupled with high replacement costs, constituted a truly formidable barrier to change. In essence, this was the point of view adopted in the Balfour Committee's *Survey of the Metal Industries*:

The British iron and steel industry [grew] up for the most part in an earlier generation, before [some of the major technological] changes were foreseen ... The necessity for writing off the heavy capital costs of the old plant, and the difficulty of raising even greater amounts of capital for the construction of new plant were serious obstacles to change. In these circumstances the process of adapting British industry to the new conditions proceeded somewhat slowly before the war. [22]

As far as sunk costs were concerned, steel makers had apparently never taken to heart Jevons's famous dictum that 'in commerce bye-gones are for ever bye-gones' [23]. Where large-scale operation and certain of the new techniques spelt enormous economies, catering to a sunk costs or 'write-off' complex (when confronting a major technological change or the necessity to enlarge the scale of operation) by permitting the continued existence of antiquated, under-sized plant would entail far greater total costs than would ensue from the replacement of existing facilities. In any case, to argue from sunk costs is really no argument at all. Far from depending on the sunk costs of the past, the decision 'to modernize an existing industry depends on the capital cost of conversion, balanced against the savings in running costs involved' [24]. But in British industry, and not least in the iron and steel industry, it often appeared that sunk costs had replaced possible 'savings in running costs' as a determining variable in the making of replacement decisions. The existing-plant argument does, however, provide an insight into the behaviour of many British industrialists, since it was a rationalization that suited the temper of those who were content to rest on their oars.

The existing-plant argument affords yet another insight into entrepreneurial behaviour if it is considered in conjunction with the problem of 'interconnectedness'. Veblen had touched upon the latter in *Imperial Germany and the Industrial Revolution* [25], and, in recent years, it has been dealt with more fully by Professor Marvin Frankel [26]. 'As an industry (or industrial economy) grows and adapts to changing and increasingly complex production methods, interconnections, more or less rigid, develop among its technological components – among machines, plant, transport network and raw material supplies – that make increasingly difficult the introduction into the system of new, cost-saving changes.' [27] In many manufacturing industries, because of the existence of a vast and complicated network of interconnections, renewal of a portion of a plant or innovation as regards a particular detail may not be worthwhile. In other words, under these circumstances, renewal or replacement will only confer major cost-reducing benefits if carried out on an 'all-or-nothing' basis – a basis which might prove to be exceedingly costly. And, to make matters more difficult, in various key British

124

industries, clusters of interconnected manufacturing operation
sometimes embraced a multitude of individual units that were each
separately owned. In such cases, therefore, major innovations would
have involved the making of decisions that cut across ownership
lines. Professor Frankel cites the slow introduction of the automatic
loom into the British cotton textile industry as a case in point [28].
Given the technical character and organization of this group of
trades at the turn of the century, a financially successful adoption of
the automatic loom would have involved the replacement of practically an entire industry. Many weaving sheds would had to have
been constructed anew. Processes antecedent to weaving would had
to have been altered. Moreover, since in Lancashire spinning and
weaving were, typically, separated with respect to ownership, much
more integration of ownership of these two phases would had to
have been effected to have reaped the full advantage of the new
device.

In general, industries starting afresh in newly industrialized
countries can avoid the deleterious effects of interconnectedness –
so runs the argument [29]. However, cotton weaving was scarcely
new to the New England of sixty years ago; yet the Northrop
automatic loom was adopted much more rapidly in New England
than in Lancashire, although, admittedly, the New England industry
was from an ownership point of view rather more integrated than
its Lancashire counterpart and hence possessed one important
characteristic that could reduce some of the difficulties associated
with interconnectedness. It is true that interconnectedness can pose
problems, but replacement of antiquated plant – for example, out-
of-date steel rolling mills – is decidedly within the realm of possibility,
given a correct attitude to sunk costs and total conversion costs (and
given, also, the ability to finance). But if the prevailing attitude to
costs is ostrich-like or incorrect, then interconnectedness can become
more a state of mind than a physical reality.

The Appearance of International Differences in Rates of Popula-
tion Increase, and the Problem of Investment and Technical Lag

Britain was not alone among major powers to undergo an eventual
abatement in that rate of increase in numbers which had made the
first half of the nineteenth century, and later decades in some
countries, stand out against all previous eras in respect of population

growth. But the eventual slowing down had begun rather earlier in Britain than in Germany and the United States. Certainly, for the entire period 1890–1913, the rate of increase in Britain was well below that of the other two countries. (See Table 13) Might this, then, be accounted another reason for Britain's technical lag *vis-à-vis* the other two powers?

TABLE 13

Population Growth, United Kingdom, Germany, and United States, 1880–1913

Year	United Kingdom		Germany		United States	
	Population (in millions)	Percentage increase	Population (in millions)	Percentage increase	Population (in millions)	Percentage increase
		%		%		%
1880	30·7	—	45·1	—	50·3	—
1890	33·9	10·4	49·2	9·9	63·1	25·4
1900	37·9	11·8	56·0	13·8	76·1	20·8
1910	41·8	10·3	64·6	15·4	92·4	21·4
1913	42·5	1·7	67·0	3·7	97·2	5·2

SOURCES: I. Svennilson, *Growth and Stagnation in the European Economy*, pp 63 and 236. US Bureau of the Census, *Historical Statistics of the United States, Colonial Times to 1957*, p 7.

It is almost a dictum in economic analysis that in advanced economies marked differences in rates of population increase will, *ceteris paribus*, eventually be reflected in significant differences in the inducement to invest (although, of course, the inducement to invest can be influenced by other phenomena as well). The relationship posited here is a direct one. A rapidly growing population will (in entrepreneurial calculations) elevate anticipated income, and, other things being equal, raise the marginal efficiency of capital, and, hence, also, the rate of investment. That the rate of capital formation in the United Kingdom lagged behind that of the United States during the 'nineties and first decade-and-a-half of the present century is evident enough (see Table 14), whatever the role of population change in this context. And not only was there a difference in rates of capital formation, but, as might be expected, investment expenditure as a proportion of national product tended to be lower in Britain than in the United States. (See Table 15).

If it be conceded that the rate of population increase does in fact affect the propensity to invest, and, furthermore, that a higher propensity to invest is normally associated with a more innovatory type of entrepreneurial behaviour than is a low propensity to invest, then the appearances of international differences in rates of population

TABLE 14

Growth of Stock of Capital Equipment, United Kingdom and United States, 1896–1912

Year	Value of stock of capital equipment (at constant prices)		Index numbers of values of stock of capital equipment[a] (1896 = 100)	
	United Kingdom (in 1912–13 pounds)	United States (in 1929 dollars)	United Kingdom	United States
	(£ millions)	($ millions)		
1896	3,018	11,707	100·0	100·0
1897	3,129	11,909	103·7	101·7
1898	3,273	12,193	108·4	104·2
1899	3,416	12,743	113·2	108·9
1900	3,562	13,484	118·0	115·2
1901	3,654	14,240	121·1	121·6
1902	3,768	15,260	124·8	130·4
1903	3,858	16,439	127·8	140·4
1904	3,963	17,130	131·3	146·3
1905	4,092	18,163	135·6	155·1
1906	4,234	19,573	140·3	167·2
1907	4,346	21,151	144·0	180·7
1908	4,358	21,553	144·4	184·1
1909	4,450	22,178	147·4	189·4
1910	4,557	23,068	151·0	197·0
1911	4,662	23,574	154·5	201·4
1912	4,789	24,622	159·7	210·3

[a] Computed from the second and third columns.

SOURCES: United States: R.W.Goldsmith, D.S.Brady, and H.Mendershausen, *A Study of Saving in the United States*, Vol. III (Princeton, Princeton University Press, 1956), p 20 ('Producer durables' [equipment]).

United Kingdom: E.H.Phelps Brown and B.Weber, 'Accumulation, Productivity, and Distribution in the British Economy, 1870–1938', *Economic Journal*, Vol. 63, June, 1953, p 286. (Estimated stock of capital goods [within given categories] other than buildings, valued at replacement cost.)

TABLE 15

Domestic Capital Formation as a Percentage of National Product,
United Kingdom and United States, 1869–1919

A. United Kingdom		
Decade	Domestic gross capital formation as a percentage of Gross National Product	Domestic net capital formation as a percentage of Net National Product
	%	%
1870–9	10·5	8·7
1880–9	9·2	7·4
1890–9	9·7	7·9
1900–9	10·6	8·8
1904–18	9·4	7·6
B. United States		
1869–78	21·7	13·9
1879–88	21·0	13·8
1889–98	22·9	14·6
1899–1908	21·5	12·8
1909–18	19·4	10·7

SOURCE: S. Kuznets, 'International Differences in Capital Formation and Financing' in *Capital Formation and Economic Growth. A Conference of the Universities – National Bureau Committee for Economic Research* (Princeton, Princeton University Press, 1955), p 62.

increase could by themselves have resulted in differences in the willingness to innovate. Colin Clark has pointed out that a rapid rate of capital accumulation is not *necessarily* to be associated with either a large measure of technical progress or a rapid rise in productivity [30]. *Net* investment may drop to low levels, but if at the same time there is active *replacement* of obsolete plant, there might still be ample scope for technological and organizational improvement [31]. However, notwithstanding the position taken by Mr Clark, a relatively rapid rate of capital accumulation will surely make the industrial environment more favourable to technical progress than a slow or negligible rate of such accumulation.

How relevant, though, is the population increase–investment–technical progress linkage to the case of Britain [32]? The population of the United Kingdom increased almost forty per cent between 1880 and 1913. Under such circumstances it can scarcely be maintained

128

that the magnitude of the population increase during this period constituted a major retardative influence. Moreover, although the rate of population increase undoubtedly has a bearing upon the rate of capital formation in any economy, it is not necessarily true that a lagging rate of capital formation is *solely* a function of a relatively slow rate of population growth. The pattern of population change can, it is true, influence not only investment behaviour but entrepreneurial behaviour generally: however, there is a hard core of such behaviour which must be considered apart from demographic factors and which has its roots in a variety of phenomena.

In the end, however, if the population question is to be examined in a context that is useful for present purposes, it should be examined in conjunction with the whole question of economic growth, and, in particular, with the way in which the growth of output can affect technical progress.

The Appearance of International Differences in Rates of Growth of Output, and the Question of Technical Lag

During that critical period 1880–1914, national product was growing more rapidly in Germany and in the United States than in Great Britain. (See Tables 16 to 21) If we attempt to relate technical lag to international differences in rates of growth of output, Britain's slower growth rate can, of course (as in the case of investment), be viewed as an effect as well as a cause. Since technological and organizational shortcomings contributed to productivity differentials,

TABLE 16

Average Annual Growth Rates of Real National Product, United Kingdom, United States and Germany, 1860–1913

	United Kingdom (1870–1913)	United States (1869/78–1913)	Germany (1860–1913)
	% per annum	% per annum	% per annum
Growth rate of real national product	2·4	4·3	3·0

SOURCE: R. W. Goldsmith, 'Financial Structure and Economic Growth in Advanced Countries: An Experiment in Comparative Financial Morphology', in *Capital Formation and Economic Growth*, p 115.

129

TABLE 17

Growth in Manufacturing Output, United Kingdom and United States, 1870–1920

Year	Output index (1870 = 100)		Percentage increase in output since preceding date		Compound percentage increase in output per annum	
	United Kingdom	United States	United Kingdom	United States	United Kingdom	United States
			%	%	%	%
1870	100·0	100·0	—	—	—	—
1880	123·3	168·6	23·3	68·6	2·2	5·5
1889	151·7	263·2	23·0	56·1	2·4	5·1
1899	175·7	398·7	15·9	51·5	1·5	4·3
1907	193·3	642·4	10·0	61·1	1·2	6·2
1920	260·4	1045·5	34·7	62·7	2·3	3·8

SOURCE: M.Frankel, *British and American Manufacturing Productivity*, p 81.

TABLE 18

Indexes of Output for Selected Industries, United Kingdom and United States; 1907 compared with 1870

Product group	Index of output in 1907 (1870 = 100)	
	United Kingdom	United States
Pig-iron	269	1,548
Refined sugar	158[a]	539
Paper	532	1,092
Distilled liquors	205[b]	241
Zinc (consumption)	268[c]	1,534
Cotton (consumption)	184	624
Rubber (consumption)	270	860
Copper (consumption)	195[d]	2,665[e]

[a] 1883   [c] 1881   [e] 1906
[b] 1898   [d] 1889

SOURCE: M.Frankel, *British and American Manufacturing Productivity*, p 82.

these shortcomings must have played a part in the appearance of growth rate differentials. But the growth rate can also affect the pace and character of technological change.

More specifically, it can be stated as a minimum hypothesis that technological advance is apt to be favoured where national product is growing rapidly than where it is not. Although growth rates in Britain were not languishing at near-stagnation levels – a better than two-and-a-half-fold increase in the physical volume of output of

TABLE 19

Rates of Increase in Iron and Steel Production, United Kingdom and Germany, 1880–1913

	United Kingdom	Germany
	(Average annual percentage rates of increase)	
Pig-iron	%	%
1880–2 to 1895–7	0·20	5·00
1895–7 to 1911–3	0·80	6·70
1880–2 to 1911–3	0·50	5·90
Steel		
1880–2 to 1895–7	5·70	11·50
1895–7 to 1911–3	3·60	8·50
1880–2 to 1911–3	4·60	9·95

SOURCE: Svennilson, *op. cit.*, p 123.

TABLE 20

Apparent Consumption of Steel (and Wrought Iron), United Kingdom, Germany, and United States, 1883–1913

Years	Average annual consumption in millions of tons			Percentage increase over preceding period		
	United Kingdom	Germany	United States	United Kingdom	Germany	United States
				%	%	%
1883–9	2·1	2·6	—	—	—	—
1890–						
1900	3·3	4·6	—	57	78	—
1901–6	4·8	7·2	18·2	48	56	—
1907–13	5·6	10·9	25·0	17	51	37

SOURCE: Svennilson, *op. cit.*, p 123.

manufactured goods during the period 1881–1913 (see Table 21) scarcely warrants such a suggestion – the fact is that the American and German economies were growing much more rapidly than the British and were therefore providing industrial milieus rather more favourable to technical and organizational advance. The differential effects in question are similar to those that are attributed to disparities in rates of population increase, except that in formal economic analysis the investment activity in the 'growth of output' case is considered to have a different originating mechanism than it does in the 'population' case. In the latter, rising investment expenditure is considered to be 'autonomous' *vis-à-vis* other macroeconomic variables; in the former it is 'induced', through the so-called 'accelerator effect', by rising income and consumption. (These two origins of investment activity are of course not mutually exclusive.) More to the point, differences in rates of growth of output or income lead to differences in the rates of increase of 'induced' investment, and, if the argument of the previous section is accepted, to differences in the will to innovate as well. Moreover, the accelerator effect aside, a slower rate of growth of output generally breeds a more cautious attitude in the entrepreneurial community: where an economy is growing rather slowly there will be a much greater emphasis upon security than upon seeking out new methods.

Implicit in the above is a view of innovating activity being stimulated by economic growth but consisting on the whole of *internal*

TABLE 21

Production and Exports of Manufactured Goods, United Kingdom, Germany, United States, and the World; 1911-1913 compared with 1881-1885

Country	Volume in 1911-1913 as a percentage of volume in 1881-1885	
	Production	Exports
	%	%
United Kingdom	162	175
Germany	363	290
United States	377	537
World	310	239

SOURCE: Svennilson, *op. cit.*, p 219.

economies, in the Marshallian sense; that is, of improvements in technique that are adopted by individual firms primarily as a result of the resources and resourcefulness of these individual firms [33]. However, the question of *external economies*, or those economies that are more directly related to growth in the aggregate output of an industry or sector of an economy than to the resources or propensity to innovate of individual entrepreneurs [34], must also be considered. The external economies especially relevant here include those opportunities for specialization of output – and, above all, opportunities for the rise of component specialists – that are directly related to the growth of an industry's output, and that industry-wide standardization which may be considered, in part, a direct consequence of the growth of output. That these tendencies were more in evidence in the United States than in Britain could no doubt be attributed in some measure to the slower rate of growth in the British economy.

Then, too, it is highly probable that differences in degree of factor mobility, including labour force mobility, will also appear as a result of differences in rates of growth of income. (Low labour mobility is not wholly socially induced.) Moreover, problems of interconnectedness will diminish in significance where rates of growth of income are high. This is because replacement on an 'all-or-nothing' basis will not involve so heavy a social cost or so heavy a risk where growth rates are high.

One aspect of economic growth that had an undeniable bearing upon the retardation problem in Britain is the matter of export growth rates. A declining trend in the rate of growth of British exports became noticeable during the eighteen-seventies. In the British context a decline in growth rates in this sector could have had a particularly deleterious effect upon the inducement to invest [35] (and the will to innovate) once the railway fever had subsided somewhat, for it was the export sector which, as a rule, had provided the greatest single fillip to bold entrepreneurship.

The Export 'Mix': An Anglo-German Comparison

Possibly as significant in the present context as export growth rates is the question of the 'mix' of the British export bill. Far-reaching attempts to capture and *maintain* commanding positions in highly competitive international markets for complex capital goods, and for the products of 'science' industries, in that they necessarily result in significant commitments of technical skill and entrepreneurial expertise to the solution of complex production and distribution problems, help to create an industrial atmosphere receptive to innovation, not only in the industries immediately affected but in other pursuits as well, and to foster constant awareness among political and economic elites of the need for adequate facilities for the development of the requisite skills. On the other hand, an export bill in which relatively simple items such as coal and cotton textiles feature most prominently does not provide much pressure or incentive for the maximum play of science, technical expertise and alert entrepreneurship. Thus, if there is already a neglect of such things as adequate facilities for technical instruction, a huge and continuing involvement in the selling abroad of coal and cotton goods might serve to help perpetuate this neglect.

On the eve of the First World War, the British and German economies were not totally dissimilar in the mix of their economic activities, and this degree of similarity was reflected to some extent in the patterns of their commodity export trade. More important, however, were the differences. (See Table 22.) Thus in Germany, in 1913, chemical exports accounted for over 14 per cent of an export aggregate which comprised coal and the principal categories of manufactured goods: this was almost three times greater than the percentage of chemicals in this same aggregate in Britain. Moreover, machinery exports, which accounted for almost 18 per cent of the German total, formed only 10 per cent of the British. At the same time, textile exports which accounted for almost half of the British aggregate, accounted for less than a quarter of the German. Finally, the relative importance of coal in the British total was almost a fifth greater than it was in the German.

Did the composition of her commodity export bill then tell against Britain in the matter of technical advance? Most probably, to some degree it did. However, is it not possible to look upon the British export mix of these pre-war years as an effect or symptom as well as a cause—a symptom of an entrepreneurship not sufficiently informed by planning horizons and forecasts that might reveal diminished marginal returns to traditional export pursuits in a not-too-distant future, nor, even if discerned, not sufficiently responsive to all of the relevant market signals? But, as already intimated, it was at the same time a symptom which aggravated the underlying disease.

TABLE 22

Percentage Distribution of the Exports of Coal and Principal Categories of Manufactured Goods, United Kingdom and Germany, 1913

Commodity Group	United Kingdom	Germany
	%	%
Coal	13·3a	11·0b
Metals	16·7	28·9
Machinery	10·0	17·7
Transport equipment	6·1	4·2
Chemicals	5·1	14·4
Textiles	48·8	23·9
Total of all the above	100·0	100·0c

a Includes, in addition to coal, coke and manufactured fuel.
b This refers to 1912 and includes, in addition to coal, coke and briquettes.
c Does not add up to 100·0 because of 'rounding'.

SOURCES: *Coal:* United Kingdom: Computed from B. R. Mitchell, *Abstract of British Historical Statistics* (Cambridge, Cambridge University Press, 1962), p. 305.

Germany: Computed from J. H. Clapham, *The Economic Development of France and Germany 1815–1914*, 4th ed. (Cambridge, Cambridge University Press, 1936), p. 283.

Other commodity groups: Computed from Svennilson, *op. cit.*, p. 294.

The Export of Capital

'Excessive' export of capital has sometimes been cited as another possible economic cause of technical lag in Britain [36] (although 'excessive' in this context has never been defined with precision). That this was in fact a partial explanation of retardation is not beyond question. For one thing, during the entire period 1880–1914 the years of the greatest relative and absolute importance of overseas investment (see Table 23) were the seven years prior to the First World War, so that the export of capital assumed its greatest importance long after a condition of relative technical lag first became apparent in British industry. In any event, it would be exceedingly difficult to prove that the export of capital had a restraining effect, either through deleterious effects on the interest rate structure or in any other way, upon real capital formation at home or prevented the achievement of a rate of domestic investment high enough to meet the needs of rapid technical change. Inspection of the interest rate structure on the London long-term capital market (see Table 24) affords no *prima facie* evidence of a dearth of loanable funds for domestic investment during those years. Nor, when we take into account a variety of supply and demand considerations, can it be demonstrated that the volume of funds for domestic investment would have been greater than it was if the export of capital had been curtailed. Thus, suppose that the outflow of capital had been stopped by administrative fiat. The *immediate* result – thinking both of supply and demand behaviour – might have been a rise in the consumption function of upper income groups at home, or an increase in idle cash balances, or in both of these things – or, indeed,

TABLE 23

Net British Domestic and Overseas Investment[a], 1871–1913

Year	Net domestic investment	Net overseas investment
	(£ millions)	(£ millions)
1871	79	57
1872	79	71
1873	94	60
1874	78	49
1875	65	26
1876	98	−4
1877	112	−16
1878	91	−3
1879	58	16
1880	91	6
1881	107	42
1882	113	33
1883	104	27
1884	56	55
1885	63	44
1886	79	75
1887	83	81
1888	118	90
1889	131	80
1890	115	95
1891	78	55
1892	76	40
1893	69	47
1894	124	23

[a] In 1912/13 £s.

136

TABLE 23 – *continued*

Year	Net domestic investment	Net overseas investment
	(£ millions)	(£ millions)
1895	147	27
1896	143	48
1897	156	32
1898	205	18
1899	220	32
1900	211	31
1901	153	14
1902	165	10
1903	147	23
1904	167	27
1905	198	66
1906	194	108
1907	153	139
1908	65	135
1909	135	113
1910	145	154
1911	128	193
1912	147	207
1913	—	212

SOURCES: Net domestic investment: E. H. Phelps Brown and S. J. Handfield-Jones, 'The Climacteric of the 1890's: A Study in the Expanding Economy', *Oxford Economic Papers* (NS), Vol. 4, Oct., 1952, p 305.

Net overseas investment: E. H. Phelps Brown and B. Weber, *op. cit.*, p 286.

TABLE 24

Rates offered by Home, Colonial and Foreign Borrowers on Large Issues on the London Long-term Capital Market, 1900–4 and 1905–9

	Home borrowers	Colonial borrowers	Foreign borrowers
	%	%	%
1900–4	3·18	3·33	5·39
1905–9	3·61	3·94	4·97

SOURCE: A. K. Cairncross, *Home and Foreign Investment 1870–1913* (Cambridge, Cambridge University Press, 1953), p 227.

anything *but* an increase of the flow of funds into domestic investment. Conceivably, there *could* have been an increase in the demand for funds for domestic investment if the reduced capital outflow resulted in downward pressure on the interest rates facing domestic investors, but, again, an increase in this demand would have been far from certain. In short, a growing volume of capital exports is by itself neither argument nor adequate reason for the slower rate of capital formation in British manufacturing industry than obtained in manufacturing industry elsewhere, or for relative technical lag, or for any of the organizational shortcomings in British industry.

The Significance of Non-Competitive Behaviour

It is a widely held belief that among the competitive pressures that will abate as a result of a tendency to concentration of ownership, monopolization, and oligopoly, or to various forms of associative activity, is the pressure to innovate [37]. It has also been alleged that Britain, of all the great industrial powers, was the main sufferer from the supposed ill effects of the propensity to monopolize and of anti-competitive behaviour generally, since non-competitive patterns had a firmer hold upon British industry than upon the industry of any other country. Neither of these beliefs is wholly admissible.

First of all, fewness of firms and the predominance of the large-scale operation, while often destructive of vigorous *price* competition – as in the case of the oligopolistic behaviour of economic theory – has frequently resulted in fiercely competitive behaviour in *non-price* areas. True, much of this competition has been confined to sterile 'selling activities' – that is, sterile from the point of view of technological advance – but not all of it; for the ploys of the oligopolist have included a constant search for productivity-increasing or cost-reducing techniques.

There is, however, one form of imperfectly competitive behaviour which is both ubiquitous and potentially hurtful to the cause of technical progress. This is the practice of constantly seeking security in price-fixing and market-sharing arrangements, either overtly or tacitly, depending upon the nature of the legal barriers present. Such arrangements were very much a part of the British industrial firmament. In spite of the hostility of the English common law to agreements in restraint of trade – although by the closing decades of the nineteenth century this hostility, in so far as the British courts were concerned, had largely evaporated [38] – and in spite of academic and party political worship of the gods of competition, a host of British industries had enjoyed long traditions of collusive action designed to restrain competition. In the eighteenth century, in both the coal and copper industries, there were associations of producers whose sole *raison d'être* was the elimination of competitive behaviour. Nor were price-fixing and similar arrangements any novelty in the iron trade. Local associations in South Staffordshire and in the Cleveland area had been fixing prices for many years. Sometimes, local collusive action was carried to extreme lengths, being eventually transformed into exceedingly tight local monopolies.

The intensity and incidence of associative, anti-competitive activity were, in all probability, cyclical in nature. The third and fourth quarters of the nineteenth century had seen the high tide of mid-Victorian prosperity came and go, and with it, no doubt, some change in the tempo of anti-competitive behaviour. The eighteen-fifties, 'sixties and early 'seventies had been years of growing aggregate demand and rising prices both at home and abroad, so that the incentive to collusive activity, although not wholly wanting – trade associations with and without market and price objectives were common during this period – was not as great as it had been during periods of falling prices and slackening demand. Then came the prolonged price fall and years of declining rates of profit that we persist in calling the 'Great Depression' (1873–96), and once again conditions were favourable to associative activity directed to controlling prices, sharing markets, and, in general, eliminating competition. What might be considered a trade association pure and simple, concerned with such things as wages and hours, legislation and trade statistics, frequently became a vehicle for price and output control. For example, during the eighteen-eighties the associations of the Cleveland and Scottish ironmasters began to attempt to regulate output (without, it would seem, any resounding success [39]).

Perhaps the most interesting examples of associative action in Britain were provided by the Birmingham 'Alliances' which had their heyday in the eighteen-nineties. The 'Alliances' even drew the local trade unions into their plans for price-fixing and local mono-poly. In return for certain stipulated wage levels and working con-ditions, the working people, through their unions, promised not to seek employment with any new firm that might try to trespass on the local monopoly [40].

It has been argued that all of this suited the British entrepreneurial temperament, a temperament which in contrast to that of the American entrepreneur found greater satisfaction and, presumably, greater psychic income, in 'co-operation' than in the fiercer varieties of price and non-price competition. But to claim that British industrialists were alone in seeking such arrangements, or that they were in any wise behind their German competitors in this respect, would be grossly inaccurate. German industry was in the thrall of anti-competitive behaviour to a far greater extent than British industry. Almost every advanced industrial country witnessed the spread of associative arrangements for fixing prices, establishing production quotas, dividing up markets, or for doing all of these things, but in no industrial country were these devices so ubiquitous or carried to such extremes of sophistication as in Germany. The German legal atmosphere was of course far more favourable to anti-competitive devices than was the British, where the courts had at one time been openly hostile to practices and agreements in restraint of trade, or the American, which had inherited the English common law tradition and which, from 1890 on, had legislation that went beyond the old common law prohibition. But even in the United States, anti-competitive arrangements were not uncommon.

The British experience with respect to anti-competitive behaviour was therefore scarcely unique. In fact, in this respect Britain was outdistanced by Germany. Yet Germany was ahead of Britain when it came to various important facets of the new industrial technology. The American propensity to collusive activity was admittedly somewhat less than the British, but was this difference in degree of sufficient magnitude to account for the considerable difference as regards technological and organizational up-to-dateness?

Confusing the Issue: The 'Tariff Reform' Debate

Joseph Chamberlain's advocacy of tariff reform moved neither Mr Balfour nor the Liberal Government, but it generated a great deal of additional interest in the question of Britain's supposed industrial lag. In the eyes of Chamberlain and his supporters the issue was simple. If there did in fact exist certain pockets of backwardness in British industry, or if it were true that there was a widespread relative decline, then this was to be attributed to the continuance of free trade. The liberal position was equally straightforward. Any weaknesses that might be found in British industry should perhaps be ascribed to entrepreneurial and other shortcomings, or anything but free trade. Indeed, far from militating against an actively innovatory behaviour in industry, free trade provides a positive spur to such behaviour – so ran the familiar liberal argument. Witness the example of shoe manufacturing. This industry, according to a liberal brief, became a factory, machine industry largely under the impetus of a heavy importation of the American machine-made product during the last decade of the nineteenth century.

Free traders who congratulated their country and themselves on this outstanding instance of the stimulating effect of free competition on a resolute industry were in order. In a time of rising prices, the value of [shoe] imports had declined over a decade (1903–13) during which that of the exports had more than doubled. The factory system [in the British boot and shoe trade] had been generalised. American methods and machinery had been adopted and adjusted to British conditions, with results satisfactory in nearly every way. [41]

The protectionists had themselves broached the matter of industrial lag; although one has the impression they were chary of tackling the question of *technological* backwardness, preferring, in most of their references to the matter of relative decline, to speak of such things as an inadequate rate of growth of national output. When, however, they were forced to confront allegations of want of enterprise in British industry, the tone they adopted was, typically, one of contempt for those who dared make such allegations. There is nothing wrong with British enterprise and British entrepreneurs, but there is a great deal wrong with British commercial policy. 'Mr Asquith thinks himself competent to lecture the chiefs of industry in this country, be they shipowners or manufacturers or agriculturalists. He knows why it is they are going behind, and not in front as quickly as they should do. He says it is want of intelligence . . . It is want of capacity, it is want of enterprise.' [42] This was Joseph Chamberlain outlining Asquith's position for the benefit of a Liverpool audience in 1903. Chamberlain, for his part, ridiculed such notions. Britain's industrial and economic woes were to be attributed to no such things, but, rather, to free trade [43].

W.A.S. Hewins was another protectionist impatient of those who offered entrepreneurial ineffectiveness as *the* reason for the alleged lag. '[Some] people argue that [in the matter of industrial progress] policy is of no importance one way or another, that it is really a question of inventions, enterprise, and the like.' [44] But 'the cheap taunts of Free Traders against the want of enterprise shown by

British business men and manufacturers' have no basis in fact [45]. This can scarcely be considered reasoned argument. Nor was it very illuminating. Although Hewins pointed to the relatively slow growth of Britain's industrial output [46], to the relative decline in iron and steel production [47], and to a general condition of 'relative back-wardness' [48], the implication is that all of this had come to pass as a result of free trade. There the matter ends, for Hewins takes us no further than the sweeping generalizations of the most self-assured of tariff reformers. In fairness to the tariff reformers, however, it should be added that the liberal position had its underpinning of blind faith, too.

The truth is that the great debate that was the 'Fiscal Question' yielded few if any real insights into the problems of industrial efficiency, entrepreneurial skill, and retardation. Typical of the confusion that could arise and of the way in which insubstantial premises could appear as dogmatic certainties in the debate over tariff reform is the following:

> One of the results of the failure of Mr Chamberlain in 1906 was a stimulus to combinations in industry . . . Manufacturers tried to obtain by combination and the allocation of markets the steadiness of trade which they could not obtain by national policy. Under the influence of these constantly extending combinations the small manufacturer now [1924] has little chance, and works after works one knew twenty years ago, running independently and prosperously on established lines, have now been swallowed up by the great industrial combinations of the last few years. [49]

What *evidence* was there for this presumed influence of free trade upon the structure of British industry? The author did not supply it. The movements he speaks of – combination, association, and the like – predated Chamberlain's failure by many, many years. Nor does he mention that from the point of view of industrial efficiency, a tendency to displace small by large-scale operations ought to have been accounted a *desideratum*, at least in some British industries.

On the related issue of price-fixing and other harmful manifestations of 'combination' – the question of desirable firm size aside – the points should probably go to the free traders. The scope and effects of price-fixing and a variety of monopoly practices would, it is not unreasonable to suppose, have been magnified rather than diminished by a stringent measure of protection and a consequent abatement of competitive pressures from abroad.

PART 4

7

Summary and Conclusion

Entrepreneurial drives and responses are the prime movers of an industrial machine. At a most fundamental level of explanation, these drives and responses come from behind the economists' veil of *ceteris paribus*. If, therefore, entrepreneurial drives were sometimes weak and responses passive where they should have been active, the ultimate source of the weakness is to be sought in the nature of the society and its institutions. In the British case, the society was essentially a conservative one, and this conservatism was an important social and social-psychological source of entrepreneurial passivity.

The conservatism was not merely a matter of undue caution or sheer inertia. There was also excessive entrepreneurial self-confidence, born of past industrial greatness and expressing itself in complacency in the face of the need to change.

These essentially conservative traits, together with certain other mores of the upper strata of British society, had at least two manifestations that were most damaging to technical progress in British industry. The first was what may be aptly termed a cult of amateurism – a cult that militated against the development of a spirit of professionalism among those who directed industry and, also, against a belief in the need for rigorous training for managers and others who served in a supervisory capacity. The second manifestation, very much bound up with the first, was the relative neglect of science in industry. The very existence of industries that could give a prominent place to amateurs, and that at the same time prospered, helped to perpetuate the myth that manufacturing industry could, on the whole, get along with relatively little close contact with scientific investigation and, also, without employing a great army of scientific personnel. Little wonder, then, that the facilities for training in the applied sciences, and for the inducement of sub-professional technical skills, left something to be desired, at least from a quantitative point of view. Underdeveloped applied science faculties in existing universities, a lack of polytechnic institutions at the university level and of higher technical schools just below the university level, and thinness on the side of the sciences in public school curricula, were perhaps all consequences of the cult of amateurism, and of entrepreneurial indifference to problems of renovating and innovating in the country's manufacturing industries.

To entrepreneurial conservatism, with its shades of self-confidence and complacency and its legacy of deleterious consequences, must be added a relatively high degree of social immobility as yet another social source of technical and organizational lag in British industry. This immobility, together with certain class-ridden notions concerning social status, showed itself, first of all, in a system of recruitment to the higher places in industry which was cloyed by class prejudice and nepotism. The recruiting base for managerial positions was therefore much narrower than it might have been. The second manifestation of social immobility and class-ridden ideas on social status had to do with levels of remuneration and income norms. Working-class wage levels – and, for that matter, managerial incomes and the returns to property – were not wholly economic quanta, determined by factor proportions and marginal productivities. Ideas concerning 'customary' wage levels, together with widely held but not always well-articulated views on income norms, were also of some importance in the determination of wage levels. That is, wage levels were, in part at least, *socially* determined – a determination, incidentally, that proceeded as much from the *workers' own views* on wage objectives as from those of the élite. And the contribution of the working classes to this determination was of such a nature as to abate what might have been a rather more vigorous striving to reach higher income goals. This is not to suggest that the British working classes were inactive on the wages front: striking out after higher wages was among the most important of trade union *raisons d'être* in Britain as elsewhere. But where the business of striking out after higher wages is apt to be circumscribed by class-ridden views on income norms, the wages pressure on management is likely to be somewhat less than it is where no such notions and traditions influence working-class behaviour. A labour force such as the British, class-conscious in the above sense, is therefore likely to provide a weaker spur to entrepreneurial alertness and the constant seeking out of cost-reducing techniques than is one whose efforts to win higher wages are not at all compromised by thinking in terms of income norms or adhering to traditional views on status. To argue, then, that entrepreneurial neglect of mechanization and of labour-saving techniques in general was primarily a function of factor supplies and relative factor prices (*vide* Habakkuk [1]), although not incorrect on formal analytical grounds, is somewhat of an over-simplification of the matter. It is no doubt true that abundance of labour inclined British entrepreneurs to the labour-intensive rather than the capital-intensive end of the spectrum of industrial techniques (in Professor Habakkuk's terms), but to end the analysis at this point is to provide less than the whole story.

A fairly high degree of social immobility, well-defined and relatively rigid attitudes to status, and a class-determined and frequently nepotic approach to the problem of recruitment to the industrial élite were not wholly unfamiliar aspects of the German industrial scene. But in Germany there were important offsets to this pattern; offsets which included a greater spirit of professionalism among the industrial élite, a greater appreciation of the need for appropriate training for this élite (and for those further down the industrial hierarchy as well), and a devotion to science and a recognition of its place within an industrial context that contrasted sharply with the British penchant for 'muddling through'.

How much weight is to be attached to trade union job- and income-protective policies as retardative factors? No universally acceptable answer to this query is possible. Yet, it must be conceded that where job-protective policies succeeded, the immediate incentive for entrepreneurs to innovate was probably less than would have been the case if such policies had failed, or, better still, if such policies had never been adopted in the first place.

As to the more purely economic causes of technical and organizational lag in British industry, there is a difficult problem of determining relative importance. For example, how important were the economic and technical consequences of Britain's relatively inferior endowment of natural resources? While international economic relationships can make good the niggardliness of nature with regard to base metals, a shortage of some of the sources of energy could not be so compensated, and could, therefore, in some instances, have played a part in inducing technical lag. Thus, it has been argued that a relative scarcity of sites for hydroelectric power development helped prevent the rapid spread of electrification in Britain. It has also been argued that absolute scarcities of petroleum and natural gas may have prevented an early and widespread adoption in Britain of certain of the newer types of prime mover. On the other hand, Britain's disadvantages with respect to sources of energy surely cannot be accepted as *the* explanation of the relatively slow spread of electrification in British industry, or of the American lead as regards the internal combustion engine.

Did Britain's relatively early start as an industrial power have unfortunate economic (and non-economic) consequences for technical progress? First, it is a fact that older plant does not lend itself so well to the introduction of new methods of industrial organization. After all, new methods of organization are usually conceived within the context of the latest physical plant. Therefore, in those industries where existing plant was out of date, many of the newer modes of industrial organization which had been devised in more up-to-date technical surroundings may have been difficult or impossible to introduce. Secondly, the mere presence of older plant and equipment may, over the years, have an unfortunate effect upon entrepreneurial attitudes.

The problem of interconnectedness can also be viewed as being in large measure a consequence of an early start, or more precisely, of a continuing maturation in the same old grooves after the early start. However, interconnectedness can sometimes be more a state of mind than a physical or economic reality, especially where entrepreneurs suffer from a sunk costs complex. Still, interconnectedness can pose real problems in the case of fabricating activities that encompass several different types of process and plant, and where, in addition, the units of ownership are, typically, coextensive with a single plant or a single process rather than with a great integrated sprawl of the latter.

One economic reason that has often been advanced for technical and organizational lag in British industry – strictly speaking, it, too, is not a purely economic reason – is the character of the market (domestic and foreign) for British goods. The familiar argument that the nature of the demands in this market took its toll when it came to the development of the various facets of the mass production technique in Britain, including, especially, standardization of product, is not to be dismissed out of hand.

Possibly the most important of all the economic factors is the slower rate of growth of Britain's national product as compared to the American growth rate (although, admittedly, Britain's slower rate of growth of output must be viewed as an effect as well as a cause of technical lag). At least three sets of consequences of the slower British growth rates should be considered. First, there is the wholly plausible assumption that a slower rate of growth of national product (and, in advanced economies, of population, too) will provide a weaker spur to the inducement to invest and the will to innovate. The investment component of national product needs to be stressed here because the rate of investment can have an obvious and important bearing on the rate of technical progress. Specifically, investment not only creates the physical capacity for further innovation and technical progress, but additional expertise as well. A related consideration that deserves mention is the slowing down of the growth rate in the export sector of the British economy. In Britain, after the abatement of the railway fever, the export sector of the economy became *the* sector for entrepreneurial daring. The reduced rate of growth that this sector suffered after the eighteen-seventies must therefore be accounted another retardative factor.

Secondly, a slower rate of growth of national product does not bring as bounteous an endowment of external economies as does a more rapid rate. This applies to all external economies but especially to the three that are of relevance to the present discussion: that is, opportunities for plant-wide specialization of product, the rise of component specialists, and opportunities for industry-wide standardization (although the slow spread of these is to be attributed to other factors as well, including the above-mentioned market and demand considerations).

Thirdly, interconnectedness will usually be a more serious problem where rates of growth of output are slower.

Finally, there is the question – at least as significant as one of the components of the growth story – of the mix of Britain's export package; a package in which textiles bulked far larger than chemicals, in which coal was more important than machines and machine tools, a package, in short, which was scarcely designed to mount the maximum pressure for technological progress and aggressive entrepreneurship. But were the contents of this mix symptom as well as cause: were they to be attributed, at bottom, to an entrepreneurship that sometimes failed to generate appropriate reactions to the signals

149

of the marketplace? Still, it was also a case of the symptom helping to feed the malady itself.

To conclude, technical and organizational lag in British industry was, more than anything else, a question of entrepreneurial responses – responses that drew their character from certain social, and social-psychological circumstances, but which were further conditioned by the economic (and other) consequences of Britain's earlier start as an industrial power, of the nature of the market for British goods, of the mix of the British export bill, and of the rate of growth of Britain's national product (with the last being possibly the most important of these). It is to be noted that important aspects of the early-start problem may be deemed social or social-psychological in nature, and that the nature of the market (especially the domestic market) for British goods was not a wholly economic phenomenon. The social well-springs of the observed technical lag can therefore acquire still greater importance *vis-à-vis* other retardative factors.

Appendix

The following were among the questions put to the members of the Mosely Commission (see *Mosely Industrial Commission to the USA, op. cit.*):

'21 (*a*) Do you consider American factories better equipped for production than English?

(*b*) Are they better managed? and are a greater proportion of University trained men employed in management than is the case in England?'

The replies to these questions were as follows:

P. Walls (*National Federation of Blastfurnacemen*):

'(*a*) Yes; very much better.

(*b*) Yes.' (p 18)

J. Maddison (*Friendly Society of Ironfounders of Great Britain and Ireland*):

'There is not a great deal of difference, but what little there is is in favour of the Americans.' (p 31)

G. N. Barnes (*Amalgamated Society of Engineers*):

'(*a*) In some respects American workshops are better equipped than English. They are equipped with a greater variety of special tools made for special work of repetition character, and on the other hand there is less range in regard to the size of tools in the workshops, and, therefore, because of that I think greater production. In this connection it should be remembered that America has 80 millions of people, with a high spending capacity, and a country constantly making fresh demands upon her industrial resources, and hence American engineers have been able to do things wholesale; in fact, they have been pressed to do so, and this has led to the adoption of plans for the manipulation of parts in a wholesale way by

151

operating upon a number at a time, and by all sorts of little contrivances for securing uniformity and despatch.

(*b*) The American manager is more enterprising and more ready to introduce the latest and best of everything, and he also works hard himself, being often himself the first in the workshop and the last out; but in justice to the English manager it ought to be said that the spirit of enterprise is more general in America, and, as I have previously stated, there is an all-round readiness to accept new ideas, and a general hankering for machinery and appliances, so that the position of the American manager is relatively easier.' (p 72)

D.C.Cummings (Iron and Steel Shipbuilders' and Boilermakers' Society):

'The equipment of shipyards and shops in other ways, that is in machinery, is not better than in Great Britain; in fact, better machinery can easily be found in the old country.' (p 86)

A.Wilkie (Associated Shipwrights' Society):

'(*a*) Speaking generally, and applying the question as to shipyards, I do not think so.

(*b*) The management required in shipyards is that of a specially trained nature, and the managers should have a practical knowledge of the work they have to supervise.' (p 100)

R.Holmshaw (Sheffield Cutlery Council):

'(*a*) Yes. There is a greater use of machinery and no expense is spared to secure any new device that will increase output.

(*b*) In the cutlery trades, yes. The work is given out systematically and no pieceworker has to waste any of his time in journeys to various parts of the factory for work, as is the case too often in Sheffield. In American factories the time of a skilled workman is too valuable to his employers to allow of its being frittered away in running about for work; hence the methodical system which sees that each man has his wants supplied by unskilled labour. Speaking generally, there seemed to be a greater proportion of trained men employed in the management than in England, and this is no doubt due to the increased facilities America has for such training.' (p 110)

T.Jones (Midland Counties Trades Federation):
'(*a*) Yes.
(*b*) More trained men employed.' (p 121)

152

T. Ashton (Operative Cotton Spinners):

'Comparing American factories with English factories, and their equipment for production, I can only say, so far as the cotton spinning industry is concerned, that the only advantage which I found to obtain in the American mills is that a much better material is used than is the case for the same counts of yarn in the English mills. I don't think the American cotton mills are better managed than the English mills, and there are very few University trained men in either country who are employed as managers. In America workmen who have attended technical schools and passed examinations in the various subjects related to their employment are given preference when promotions have to be made.' (p 137)

W. H. Wilkinson (Northern Counties Amalgamated Association of Weavers):

'(*a*) American cotton mills are well equipped, the employers, so far as I could see, going in for the best machinery they can get.

(*b*) It is a matter of opinion whether the American mills are better managed than our English mills.' (p 146)

T. A. Flynn (Amalgamated Society of Tailors):

'(*a*) No money is spared in the equipment of American factories; the best only is good enough. Production is correspondingly increased and ensured.

(*b*) American employers interest themselves in the management of their business to a greater and more intimate extent than is the custom in England. How far University men are employed in factories I am unable to state, not having been able to obtain enough information on that point.' (p 157)

W. B. Hornidge (National Union of Boot and Shoe Operatives):

'(*a*) Some are, and, on the other hand, many are not; the employers in America do not hesitate to invest in new machinery, and if it does not come up to expectations they put it aside. Any fresh idea is worked for all it is worth.

(*b*) It is questionable whether they are better managed, in our trade, than our better factories. English employers have during the last few years generally made vast improvements in the direction of management.' (p 166)

G. J. Lapping (Amalgamated Society of Leather Workers):

'(*a*) Yes.

(*b*) Yes.' (p 173).

H. R. Taylor (Operative Bricklayers' Society):
  '(*a*) Those I have seen, yes.
  (*b*) They are better managed.' (p 183).

M. Deller (National Association of Operative Plasterers):
  '(*a*) Yes. Greater space is also given to work in.
  (*b*) I should say the organisation in an American factory is better than at home.' (p 192)

H. Crawford (General Union of Operative Carpenters and Joiners):
  '(*a*) Their appliances are much better than ours.
  (*b*) I could not say unless I really worked in the shops, but all that I consider the best methods were adopted of pushing out the work quickly. I know at home that often it is not [the] fault of the management but the niggardlines of the employers, who will not supply the best machinery to do the work. Employers in America vie with each other to get the latest up-to-date machines.' (p 202)

H. Ham (National Amalgamated Furnishing Trades' Association):
  '(*a*) Yes.' (p 212)

W. Dyson (Amalgamated Paper Makers' Union):
  '(*a*) Yes.
  (*b*) No, I don't think so. The majority of managers I met in the paper mills were men who had risen from the ranks, and, though not University trained, their standard of education was much higher than in England.' (p 218)

C. W. Bowerman (London Society of Compositors):
  '(*a*) In some respects I am inclined to believe that American printing offices are better equipped for production, in the shape of labour-saving appliances, than is the case in the general run of offices elsewhere.
  (*b*) With regard to the question whether the factories are better managed, or a greater proportion of University-trained men employed in management than is the case in England, the system appears to be to appoint none but practical men as heads of departments, which, from a business point of view, should naturally be an advantage.' (p 230)

G. D. Kelley (Amalgamated Society of Lithographic Printers):
  '(*a*) Yes.
  (*b*) Not in my trade.' (p 240)

W. Coffey (London Consolidated Society of Journeymen Bookbinders):
'With regard to the equipment of factories there is strong desire on the part of the Americans to keep pace with modern requirements. He is much helped towards the realisation of this desire by the fact of buildings being put up to a much greater height than is usual with us. Works can be planned on a more comprehensive scale. More space being secured for the various operations, men are unhampered by the common difficulty experienced here of being, at times of pressure especially, unable to find room to properly place their work. Beyond this orderly arrangement I did not observe any indications of better management. The foremen, and in many cases the employers, are men who have risen from the grade of the ordinary journeyman.' (p 251)

W. C. Steadman (TUC Parliamentary Committee):
'(*a*) In some, yes; in others, no.
(*b*) Yes.' (p 262)

Notes

CHAPTER 1

1 M. Beer, *A History of British Socialism*, Vol. 2 (London, Allen & Unwin, 1948), p 346.

2 The following brief account of the second industrial revolution is drawn largely from A. L. Levine, *Industrial Change and Its Effects upon Labour 1900–14* (Unpublished doctoral dissertation, University of London, 1954), Chapter 1.

3 One of the more astute of contemporary observers who deliberated upon the new industrial order thought he saw in the economies of advancing mechanization *the* factor which was furthering the three tendencies that, according to him, were making the eighteen-eighties and 'nineties a new era in industrial history. 'It is . . . quite evident,' he wrote in 1894, 'that economies of machinery and power are operating in many fields of industry—

1. To increase the size of individual "plant" and "establishment", employing a larger co-operative unit of capital and labour to produce a larger "output".

2. To increase the size and importance of capital in comparison to labour.

3. To produce greater differentiation and specialization of capital and labour, so as to give increased complexity to the business-unit.' (J. A. Hobson, *The Evolution of Modern Capitalism*, Revised ed. [London, Allen & Unwin, 1949], p 126.)

4 The motor trade also provided a great impetus to the invention and development of valve-grinding and hydraulic bushing machines. (See *The Engineer*, 25 May 1909, p 532.)

5 'Technology and Industrial Organization', in C. Singer *et al* (eds.), *A History of Technology*, Vol. 5 (Oxford, Clarendon, 1958), pp 807–8.

6 A. Shadwell, *op. cit.*, p 108.

7 *Ibid.*

8 See D. L. Burn, 'The Genesis of American Engineering Competition, 1850–70', *Economic History*, Vol. 2, Jan. 1933, pp 292–3; and *New York Industrial Exhibition Special Reports of Mr George Wallis and*

Mr Joseph Whitworth, Parliamentary Papers, 1854, Vol. XXXVI [74].

9 D.L.Burn, *ibid.* See, also, the *Report of the Committee on the Machinery of the United States of America*, Parliamentary Papers, 1854–5, Vol. L.

10 J.Cox of the Associated Iron and Steel Workers of Great Britain, writing in Mosely Industrial Commission to the USA, *op. cit.*, p 41.

11 *Ibid.*

12 Royal Commission on the Depression of Trade and Industry, *Second Report, Minutes of Evidence and Appendix*, Part I [Cd. 4715] 1886, p 344 (written statement by Sir Lowthian Bell).

13 J.S.Jeans, 'The British Iron and Steel Industries: Their Condition and Outlook' (1902), in W.J.Ashley (ed.), *British Industries* (London, Longmans, 1907), p 19.

14 The debate of course continues today. For a defensive account written in our own day, see J.Jewkes, 'Is British Industry Inefficient?', *Manchester School*, Vol. 14, Jan. 1946, pp 1–16.

15 'The Iron and Steel Trades Outlook', *The Economist*, 16 February 1907, p 287.

16 'Steel Trade Prospects', *The Economist*, 21 September 1907, p 1579.

17 By productivity is meant output per annum per occupied member of the labour force.

18 D.J.Coppock, 'The Climacteric of the 1890's: A Critical Note', *Manchester School*, Vol. 24, Jan. 1956, pp 23–4.

19 F.W.Taussig, 'Labour Costs in the United States Compared with Costs Elsewhere', *Quarterly Journal of Economics*, Vol. 39, Nov. 1924, pp 103–7. (Taussig's data, which relate to physical output per person employed, were based on unpublished material provided by A.W.Flux. The British estimates of physical productivity were for the year 1907 and the American for 1909.)

20 M.Frankel, *op. cit.*, p 29. Frankel's estimates of the rates of change in productivity in British and American manufacturing industry yield a ratio of 1·46 in 1870. By extrapolation this becomes 1·34 in 1860, 1·22 in 1850, 1·12 in 1840, and 1·01 in 1830.

21 *Ibid.*, p 27.

22 Cp. W.E.G.Salter, *Productivity and Technical Change* (Cambridge, Cambridge University Press, 1960), pp 98 and 162.

23 F.W.Taussig, *op. cit.*, p 105. The British figure is for 1907, the American for 1909.

24 See S.Fabricant, 'Study of the Size and Efficiency of the American Economy', in E.A.G.Robinson (ed.), *Economic Consequences of the Size of Nations* (London, Macmillan, 1960), p 46.

25 See Table 5, below.

26 *Op. cit.*, p 6.

27 *Op. cit.*, p 44. In all but two of these industries – cured fish and manufactured ice – output per worker was higher in America.

28 Rostas, *op. cit.*, p 53. See, also, *ibid.*, pp 54, and 69–70 (Table 17).

29 Cp. R.M.Solow, 'Technical Change and the Aggregate Production Function', *Review of Economics and Statistics*, Vol. 39, Aug. 1957, pp 312–20; and 'Investment and Technical Progress', in K.J.Arrow, S.Karlin, and P.Suppes, *Mathematical Methods in the Social Sciences, 1959* (Stanford, Stanford University Press, 1960), pp 89–104.

30 *Op. cit.*, p 51.

31 Cp. Salter, *op. cit.*, pp 128–30.

32 See J.Jewkes, *op. cit.*, pp 4–5.

33 Cp. Frankel, *op. cit.*, pp 13–14.

34 Gross value rather than value added has been used because the American value added figures include various 'mill supplies' used in the productive process. Although the use of gross value rather than value added introduces the problem of 'double-counting' or, more precisely, the possibility that the double-counting might have different effects in the case of the British and American data, some light may still be thrown on the central issue of the Anglo-American capital productivity *relationship*.

35 See Table 2.

36 However, the omission is not a serious one in percentage terms.

37 *Op. cit.*, Table A, p 6.

38 See W.Duane Evans, 'Economic Development: Case Studies – Discussion', *American Economic Review*, Vol. 46, May 1955, p 116.

39 It will be recalled that Chamberlain failed to get the appointment of a royal commission to examine the tariff issue. He succeeded, however, in selling the idea to a number of industrialists and others, and his advocacy resulted in the setting up of the so-called 'Tariff Commission', without government sponsorship.

40 *The Engineer* reproduced several of these papers in their entirety, and in addition, abstracted many others.

CHAPTER 2

1 This measure of mechanization is admittedly not entirely accurate, since in addition to mechanization *per se*, the *size* of the equipment in use will also have a bearing on the horsepower/worker ratio (although in some cases, the size of the equipment used could conceivably be correlated, in a rough way, with the extent to which handwork had been eliminated and hence also with the degree of mechanization).

2   F.W.Taussig, making use of data for 1907 (UK) and 1909 (US) for pig-iron making and flour milling, shows that in pig-iron making the horsepower per worker in the United States was more than twice what it was in the United Kingdom, and in flour milling over two-and-a-half times as great. (*Op. cit.*, pp 104 and 107.) Table 5, below, should also be consulted.

3   Mosely Industrial Commission to the USA, *op. cit.*, p 104.

4   *Ibid.*, p 114.

5   *Ibid.*, p 74.

6   *Ibid.*, pp 150 and 151.

7   *Annual Report of the Chief Inspector of Factories and Workshops for the Year 1914* [Cd. 8051] 1915, p 37.

8   T.H.Burnham and G.O.Hoskins, *Iron and Steel in Britain 1870–1930* (London, Allen & Unwin, 1943), pp 149 and 190. See, also, *The Engineer*, 5 November 1909, p 483.

9   See E.C.Amos, 'Portable Pneumatic Tools', *The Engineer*, 30 March 1900, p 315. See, also, the comparison made with contemporary American shipbuilding practice by D.C.Cummings of the United Society of Boiler Makers and Iron and Steel Shipbuilders in the Mosely Industrial Commission to the USA, *op. cit.*, p 80.

10 G.E.Barnett, 'The Introduction of the Linotype', in J.R.Commons (ed.), *Trade Unionism and Labor Problems* (Boston, Ginn, 1905), p 250.

11 See *The Engineer*, 15 August 1902, p 156, and 19 June 1908, p 645. See, also, A.Saxon's presidential address to the Manchester Association of Engineers (summarized in *The Engineer*, 22 January 1904, p 96).

12 *The Engineer*, Supplement, 26 November 1909, 'Grinding Machines', p i.

13 See H.I.Brackenbury, 'Modern Machinery and Its Future Development', a paper read to the British Association in 1907 (reprinted in *The Engineer*, 23 August 1907, p 221).

14 The ring-frame, although conferring the advantages of higher productivity and lesser demands on the skill of the operative, was, however, not yet as suitable as the mule for the production of finer weft threads. (See D.A.Farnie, 'The Textile Industry: Woven Fabrics', in C.Singer *et al* (eds.), *op. cit.*, Vol. 5, p 578.)

15 Cf. Shadwell, *op. cit.*, p 120.

16 Mosely Industrial Commission to the USA, *op. cit.*, pp 210 and 213. See, also, Royal Commission on Labour, *Answers to Schedules of Questions, Group 'C'* [Cd. 6795–ix] 1892; and E.A.Pratt, *Trade Unionism and British Industry* (London, Murray, 1904), p 162.

17 Mosely Industrial Commission to the USA, *op. cit.*, p 202.

18 A.Shadwell, 'History of Industrialism', in *An Encyclopaedia of Industrialism* (London, Nelson, 1913), p 299.

19   Cf. P. V. Vernon, 'Automatic Lathe Work', *The Engineer*, 18 November 1910, p 553.

20   'In machine tool work, progress along automatic lines has perhaps been somewhat slow, probably on account of the great variety of products to be dealt with' and, also, on account of 'the absence of specialization by individual manufacturers . . . and the fact that the quantities in many cases were only small.' (*Ibid.*)

21   Cp. Shadwell, *Industrial Efficiency*, p 78.

22   Mosely Industrial Commission to the USA, *op. cit.*, p 42.

23   *Ibid.*, p 170. However, the representative of the Northern Counties Amalgamated Association of Weavers thought that as far as his industry was concerned the opposite was the case. In his opinion, the speeds at which looms were run in America were 'considerably less than is the case in this country'. (*Ibid.*, p 143.)

24   1919 ed. (London, Bell), p 323.

25   *Op. cit.*, p 198.

26   *The Engineer*, 8 February 1901, p 143.

27   P 345.

28   J. H. Clapham, *Economic History of Modern Britain*, Vol. 3, *Machines and National Rivalries, 1887–1914* (Cambridge, Cambridge University Press, 1938), p 156.

29   See, for example, the Appendix to the reports of the members of the Mosely Commission.

30   8 July 1904, p 32.

31   *The Engineer*, 12 September 1902, p 253.

32   *Op. cit., loc. cit.*

33   [Cd. 9072] 1918.

34   For an account of the alleged influence of 'unfavourable' legislation, see E. Garcke, *The Progress of Electrical Enterprise* (London, Electrical Press, 1907), p 78.

35   *Op. cit.*, p 8.

36   *Report of the Departmental Committee Appointed by the Board of Trade to Consider the Position of the Iron and Steel Trades After the War* [Cd. 9071] 1918, p 5.

37   For a comparative cost argument in favour of hematite, consult the evidence offered by Sir Lowthian Bell to the Royal Commission on the Depression of Trade and Industry, *Second Report*, *Minutes of Evidence*, Part I, p 43, nos. 1960 and 1961. Sir Lowthian's evidence is not, however, altogether convincing.

38   G. C. Allen, *British Industries and Their Organization*, 3rd ed. (London, Longmans, 1951), p 119.

39   *Ibid.*

40 Cf. W.A.Lewis, 'International Competition in Manufactures', *American Economic Review*, Vol. 67, May 1957, p 584.

41 See below, pp 53–4.

42 Cf. [Balfour] Committee on Industry and Trade, *Survey of the Metal Industries* (1928), pp 8–9; and Burnham and Hoskins, *op. cit.*, p 39.

43 Cf. Burnham and Hoskins, *op. cit.*, p 191.

44 *Ibid.*

45 'In 1913, out of some 21,000 [coke-making] ovens in use . . . only 6,000 were by-product recovery ovens . . .' [Balfour] Committee on Industry and Trade, *Factors in Industrial and Commercial Efficiency*, Part II (1928), p 159.

46 *Survey of the Metal Industries*, p 8.

47 Burnham and Hoskins, *op. cit.*, p 185.

48 Cf. D.L.Burn, *The Economic History of Steelmaking 1867–1939* (Cambridge, Cambridge University Press, 1940), pp 184, 193, 198. See, also, *The Engineer*, 5 November, 1909, p 483.

49 D.L.Burn, *The Economic History of Steelmaking*, p 191.

50 Mosely Industrial Commission to the USA, *op. cit.*, pp 46–7.

CHAPTER 3

1 Mosely Industrial Commission to the USA, *op. cit.*, p 41.

2 *Ibid.*, p 247.

3 *Ibid.*, p 169.

4 Royal Commission on the Poor Laws and Relief of Distress, Appendix Vol. IX, *Minutes of Evidence* [Cd. 5086] 1910, p 183.

5 P 3.

6 H.I.Brackenbury, *op. cit.*, p 220.

7 Mosely Industrial Commission to the USA, *op. cit.*, pp 86 and 94. It should not be thought that a high level of productive efficiency called *only* for subdivision of manufacturing processes and the use of specialized or single-purpose machines, or that such subdivision and the development of specialized appliances would, in every instance, have been the desired trend. Sometimes, depending upon the technics of production involved, an efficient arrangement of productive operations might demand the integrating of related operations on the same premises accompanied by the introduction of multipurpose machines.

8 G.C.Allen, *The Industrial Development of Birmingham and the Black Country 1860–1927* (London, Allen & Unwin, 1929), p 303.

9 *Report of the Departmental Committee Appointed by the Board of Trade to Consider the Position of the Engineering Trades After the War* [Cd. 9073] 1918, p 10.

10 *Ibid.*

11   See G.C.Allen, *British Industries and Their Organization*, p 108.

12   Burnham and Hoskins, *op. cit.*, p 43.

13   See Part 3.

14   P.S.Florence, *The Logic of Industrial Organization* (London, Kegan Paul, 1933), p 14.

15   Cp. Mosely Industrial Commission to the USA, *op. cit.*, p 74.

16   *Report of the Departmental Committee . . . [on] the Engineering Trades After the War*, p 11.

17   *Ibid.*, p 10.

18   *The Economist*, 24 January 1903, p 153. See, also, W.L.Hichens, *Some Problems of Modern Industry* (London, Nisbet, 1918), p 50.

19   *The Engineer*, 9 February 1900, pp 148–9.

20   See British Standards Institution, *Fifty Years of British Standards 1901–1951* (London, 1951), p 27.

21   *The Engineer*, 21 June 1901, p 648.

22   Soon, however, its various proposals for standardization went far beyond steel sections.

23   *Report of the Departmental Committee . . . [on] the Iron and Steel Trades After the War*, p 43.

24   See H.J.Marshall, 'Gauges and Standards as Affecting Shop and Manufacturing Administration' (a paper read to the Conference of the Institution of Civil Engineers in 1903 and summarized in *The Engineer*, 19 June 1903, p 628).

25   J.Wolfe Barry, 'Standardisation in British Engineering Practice', *The Mechanical Engineer*, 1 September 1906, p 285.

26   *The Engineer*, 31 January 1902, p 123.

27   See *The Engineer*, 26 April 1901, p 435.

28   A.Marshall, *Principles of Economics*, 8th ed. (London, Macmillan, 1938), p 257.

29   *The Basic Industries of Great Britain* (London, Benn, 1927), p 84.

30   H.F.L.Orcutt, 'Modern Machine Methods', *The Engineer*, 24 January 1902, p 97.

31   *Ibid.*

32   See, for instance, W.Arnold, 'The Engineer and the Economical Development of Manufactories', *The Engineer*, 31 August 1900, p 224.

33   See the Engineering Standards Committee, *Report on British Standard Systems of Limit Gauges for Running Fits*, Publication No. 27, June 1906.

34   Orcutt, *op. cit., loc. cit.*

35   This opinion is cited in Sidney Webb, *The Works Manager To-Day* (London, Longmans, 1918), p 134.

36   See, for instance, W.Arnold, 'The Engineer and the Economical

Development of Manufactories' (31 August 1900, p 224); E.C. Amos, 'Workshop Practice at the Beginning of the Twentieth Century' (15 March 1901, p 276); H.F.L. Orcutt, 'Modern Machine Methods' (24 January 1902, p 123); H.J. Marshall, 'Gauges and Standards as Affecting Shop and Manufacturing Administration' (19 June 1903, p 628); 'Some Milling Operations' (15 January 1904, pp 62–3); and a review of J.V. Wordsworth's *American Tool Making and Interchangeable Manufacturing* (12 January 1906, p 32).

37 H.J. Thompson, 'Jigs and Fixtures', *Proceedings of the Institution of Mechanical Engineers*, December 1914, p 983.

38 P 244.

39 Cited in Sidney Webb, *The Works Manager To-day*, p 134.

40 *History of the Ministry of Munitions* (London, 1922), Vol. IV, p 74.

41 Although the technique of mass production demands standardization, it does not necessarily demand *industry-wide* standardization, either of finished products or of component parts. Alfred Marshall's 'particular standardisation' (see his *Industry and Trade*, 4th ed. [London, Macmillan, 1921], p 201) – that is, standardization on a plant- or firm-wide basis – will usually suffice. This applies especially to interchange-ability. As we have already seen, standardization of components, where it was practised, was ordinarily (with some exceptions) on a plant-rather than on an industry-wide basis.

42 W. Mosses, in his *History of the United Pattern Makers' Association* (London, 1922), wrote that in 1913 'an American firm [was] engaged in mass production [*sic*] of motorcars at Manchester'. Thus, Mosses, writing in 1922, applies the term, 'mass production', to a phenomenon he had observed before the war. However, I have been unable to find this term actually used during the pre-war period in either *The Engineer* or the Amalgamated Engineers' *Monthly Journal*. Moreover, Hobson did not use the expression in his *Evolution of Modern Capitalism*, the first edition of which appeared in 1894, nor did Marshall in his *Industry and Trade*, written at the close of the war. Marshall does speak of 'massive production' (*Industry and Trade*, pp 55 *et seq.*), but he appears to have given the term 'massive production' a wholly quantitative significance when he elsewhere describes what we would consider to be facets of the mass production technique.

43 *History of the Ministry of Munitions, loc. cit.*

44 Cf. P.S. Florence, *op cit.*, pp 18–20; and Allyn Young, 'Increasing Returns and Economic Progress', *Economic Journal*, Vol. 38, December 1928, pp 532–3. See, also, L. Rostas, *op. cit.*, pp 58 and 61; and E. Rothbarth, 'Causes of the Superior Efficiency of USA Industry as Compared with British Industry', *Economical Journal*, Vol. 56, Sept. 1946, p 387. For points of view (and statistical data)

frequently omitted from the usual statement of the case for economies of scale, see M.Frankel, *British and American Manufacturing Productivity*; J.M.Blair, 'Technology and Size', *American Economic Review*, Vol. 38, May 1948, pp 121–52; S.Fabricant, 'Study of the Size and Efficiency of the American Economy', in E.A.G.Robinson (ed.), *Economic Consequences of the Size of Nations* (London, Macmillan, 1960); J.Jewkes, 'Are Economies of Scale Unlimited?', *ibid.*; and C.D.Edwards, 'Size of Markets, Scale of Firms, and the Character of Competition', *ibid.*

45 *Op. cit., loc. cit.*

46 It would then become possible 'to manufacture each class of apparatus in the most suitable factory, the management of which would be concentrated on its own specialty instead of being wasted in a variety of products'. (*Ibid.*)

47 In 1900, there were ten steel producers in Germany with annual capacities of over 300,000 tons; in Britain there was only one. (T.H.Burnham and G.O.Hoskins, *op. cit.*, p 42. See, also, *ibid.*, pp 233 and 269.) Secondary processes in the industry were in a similar situation. See, for example, the implied admission in the evidence submitted by the Iron and Steel Wire Manufacturers' Association to the Iron and Steel Trades Committee when the wire manufacturers complained of 'large manufacturing units' in the United States driving British firms out of various export markets. (*Report of the Departmental Committee . . . [on] the Iron and Steel Trades After the War*, p 12.)

48 *Report of the Departmental Committee . . . [on] the Engineering Trades After the War*, p 8.

CHAPTER 4

1 In formal economic analysis a distinction between 'entrepreneurship' and 'management' should usually be maintained, but this distinction may be legitimately blurred when, as in the present discussion, the focus is upon industrial technique and organization rather than upon the narrower context of formal economic analysis. Moreover, in the manufacturing industry of sixty and seventy years ago, decision-making in the realm of technique and organization was, not infrequently, a joint entrepreneurial–managerial effort, both in sole proprietorships and joint stock enterprises. It may still be so today (although the existence of the corporate behemoth does pose the problem of the location of the entrepreneurial function within the firm). More important, however, is the fact that roughly the same set of

social determinants of business and administrative behaviour was applicable to entrepreneurs and senior managers.

2 P 64.

3 Mosely Industrial Commission to the USA, *op. cit.*, p 169.

4 *Ibid.*, p 72.

5 *Ibid.*, p 157.

6 Here, however, some of the brief references to Britain's failure to remain abreast of the strides being taken by German and American competitors end on a note of confidence and national pride: 'the national character is again showing itself in a resolute facing of difficulties'. (*Industry and Trade*, 2nd ed., p 92.)

7 *Principles of Economics*, 8th ed., pp 298–300.

8 P 21.

9 *Industrial Efficiency*, p 552.

10 *Ibid.*, p 82.

11 Vol. 224, October 1916, pp 375–6.

12 The series was published in *The Times* during the course of 1901 and 1902. Subsequently, it appeared in book form under the title, *Trade Unionism and British Industry* (*op. cit.*).

13 *Ibid.*, p 157.

14 *The Engineer*, 19 April 1901, p 400.

15 These were the lectures that were published under the title, *The Works Manager To-day*.

16 Quoted in S.Webb, *The Works Manager To-day*, p 134.

17 The literature pertaining to the early phase of the scientific management movement is voluminous. In addition to F.W.Taylor's *Shop Management* (New York, Harper, 1911) and *The Principles of Scientific Management* (New York, Harper, 1913), see R.F.Hoxie, *Scientific Management and Labor* (New York, Appleton, 1918), C.B.Thompson, *The Theory and Practice of Scientific Management* (Cambridge, Houghton Mifflin, 1917), and H.B.Drury, *Scientific Management. A History and Criticism*, 2nd ed. (New York, Columbia, 1918).

18 See L.Urwick and E.F.L.Brech, *The Making of Scientific Management*, Vol. 2 (London, Management Publications Trust, 1946), p 162.

19 *Ibid.*, p 91. *The Engineer* reprinted Taylor's paper in its entirety.

20 Urwick and Brech, *op. cit.*, Vol. 2, p 162.

21 *Proceedings* of the Institution of Mechanical Engineers, 1910, p 1002.

22 *Ibid.*, pp 1008–9.

23 *Ibid.*, p 1009.

24 *Reconstruction Problems*, No 28 (London, HMSO, 1919), p 14.

25 *Ibid.*

26 *Factory Efficiency. How to Increase Output, Wages, Dividends and Good-will*, 2nd ed., London, The Efficiency Magazine, 1918.

27 2nd ed. revised, Manchester, The Scientific Publishing Co., 1905.

28 Cf. H.B.Drury, *op. cit.*, p 17.

29 *Ibid.*

30 The author of a review of the first edition of Drury's book which appeared in the *New Statesman* for 19 June 1916, commented that although a spate of newspaper articles and pamphlets dealing with scientific management had appeared in the United States following the ICC hearings of 1910, 'very few of them reached this country'.

31 See Urwick and Brech, *op. cit.*, Vol. 2, p 98.

32 P 520.

33 12 April 1912, p 382.

34 P 443.

35 *Ibid.*

36 14 November 1913, p 521.

37 *Ibid.*

38 *Ibid.*

39 London, Longmans.

40 P 168.

41 P 169.

42 P 201.

43 *Ibid.* This, of course, was the whole point: too many factory administrations in Britain were lacking in 'strenuousness'.

44 29 May 1914, p 597. (Italics added.)

45 *Ibid.* In all fairness, it should be pointed out that *The Engineer* had previously concurred in the usefulness of rigorously systematized work methods for the manufacture of articles assembled from standardized components, such as sewing machines and typewriters. However, this concession was coupled with the warning that where managers have to tackle production problems which 'vary from day to day in almost every particular', 'too much science and too rigorous systematisation of method ... is likely to lead to a decrease of efficiency rather than an increase'. (*The Engineer*, 25 April 1913, p 443.)

46 G.D.H.Cole, *The Payment of Wages* (London, Allen & Unwin, 1918), p 77.

47 'Scientific Management', *The Sociological Review*, July 1913, p 203. 'So far ... as initiative, interest, variation, experiment, and personal responsibility are factors of human values, qualifying the human costs of labour, it seems evident that Scientific Management involves a loss or injury to the workers.' (*Ibid.*, p 205.)

48 *Ibid.*, p 211.

49 *Ibid.*, p 200.

50 *Ibid.* '[But] when we pass from technical improvements of tools to

improved methods of working, we open possibilities of opposition between the business and the human interest.' (*Ibid.*, p 201.)

51 S.Webb, *The Works Manager To-day*, p 133.

52 *Ibid.*, p 136.

53 *Ibid.*, p 137.

54 Quoted in Urwick and Brech, *op. cit.*, Vol. 2, p 100.

55 Cadbury delivered a paper on 'Some Principles of Industrial Organization: the Case For and Against Scientific Management' to the Sociological Society in November 1913. (It was published in the *Sociological Review* in April 1914.) Among those who took part in the discussion that followed were J.A.Hobson, G.D.H.Cole, Walter Hazell (of Hazell, Watson and Viney, Ltd), and G.C.Renold and W.H.Jackson of Hans Renold, Ltd. (See, also, Urwick and Brech, *op. cit.*, Vol. 2, p 101.)

56 P 11.

57 C.B.Thompson, *op. cit.*, p 39.

58 E.Cadbury, *op. cit.*, p 112.

59 *Ibid.*

60 *The Sociological Review*, April 1914, p 122.

61 See D.F.Schloss, *Methods of Industrial Remuneration*, 3rd ed. (London, Williams and Northgate, 1898), p 15 n.; H.B.Drury, *op. cit.*, p 76; and E.T.Elbourne, 'The Technique of Factory Administration', *The Accountant*, 14 April 1928.

62 See, for example, the Amalgamated Engineers' *Monthly Journal*, July 1901, p 3; February 1903, p 171; May 1903, p 67; and the Amalgamated Engineers' *Report and Monthly Record*, January 1907, p 28.

63 Under the premium bonus system, a basis time, or time allowance, was calculated for each job or task. If the worker completed the task in less than the time allowed for it, he received, in addition to his standard time wages, a bonus in the form of a payment for a portion of the time he saved in executing the work.

64 *Report of an Enquiry by the Board of Trade into the Earnings and Hours of Workpeople of the United Kingdom. VI – Metal, Engineering and Shipbuilding Trades in 1906* [Cd. 5814] 1911, pp 64–5.

65 *Report of the Trades Union Congress Joint Committee on the Premium Bonus System* (Manchester, 1910), p 11.

66 *Ibid.*, pp 7 and 15.

67 See G.D.H.Cole, *The Payment of Wages*, rev. ed. (London, Allen & Unwin, 1928), pp 62 and 72. W.F.Watson, in his *The Worker and Wages Incentives* (London, Woolf, 1934), recorded that he 'struck Scientific Management at Thorneycroft's, Chiswick, in 1905. Hitherto, if a man deposited his check in the timekeeper's box within five minutes after starting-time, he could walk leisurely to his shop. Time

recorders were installed in each department and we had to "clock in" within two minutes . . .

'Charts indicating the feeds and speeds to be employed were fixed to every machine, and "feed and speed" bosses, armed with feedometers, endeavoured to keep men and machines working to their fullest capacity . . .' (p 11)

But all of this is surely nothing more than implementation of those advanced management practices that Renold and other employers had welcomed and trade unionists decried – but practices which were quite a few removes from out-and-out Taylorism.

68   E. Rothbarth, *op. cit.*, p 385. See, also, W. L. Hichens, *op. cit.*, p 50; and W. A. Lewis, *op. cit.*, p 584.

69   Reprinted in *The Engineer*, 24 November 1911, p 546.

70   *The Engineer*, 22 December 1911, p 64.

71   A. Shadwell, *Industrial Efficiency*, p 71.

72   Royal Commission on the Depression of Trade and Industry, *Second Report, Minutes of Evidence and Appendix*, Part I, p 345.

73   For an opinion on such attitudes in the British steel industry, see W. A. Lewis, *op. cit.*, p 584.

74   A. A. Young, *op. cit.*, p 535.

75   *Op. cit., loc. cit.*

76   *Ibid.*, p 21.

77   *Ibid.* See p 58, above, for the complete quotation.

78   *Incentives in the New Industrial Order* (London, Leonard Parsons, 1922), p 62.

79   *Ibid.*, p 81. See, also, W. A. Lewis, *op. cit.*, p 584.

80   See *The Neglect of Science. The Report of a Conference Held . . . [at] Burlington House, 3rd May 1916* (London, Harrison & Sons, 1916).

81   *The Neglect of Science*, p 46.

82   E. B. Poulton, Hope Professor of Zoology, *ibid.*, p 27. In support of his contention, Poulton cited the instance of slowness in developing a type of steel helmet that would afford protection against shrapnel.

83   *Ibid.*, p 44.

84   Cf. Marshall's letter, *ibid.*, p 46.

85   J. N. Lockyer, *Education and National Progress*, quoted in D. S. L. Cardwell, *The Organization of Science in England* (London, Heinemann, 1957), p 147.

86   Quoted in Cardwell, *op. cit.*, p 158.

87   Second Report of the Royal Commission on Technical Instruction, 1884; quoted in Cardwell, *op. cit.*, p 104.

88   Royal Commission on the Depression of Trade and Industry, *Second Report, Minutes of Evidence and Appendix*, Part I, p 344.

89   Cp. Hobson, *Incentives in the New Industrial Order*, p 90.

90   For an account of the social origins of manufacturers in the steel hosiery industries in Britain during the latter half of the nineteenth century and first decades of the present century, see C.Erickson, *British Industrialists, Steel and Hosiery 1850–1950* (Cambridge, Cambridge University Press, 1959), chaps. 2 and 4.

91   Hobson, *Incentives in the New Industrial Order*, p 90.

92   Reprinted in J.R.Commons (ed.), *Trade Unionism and Labor Problems* (Boston, Ginn, 1905), p 290.

93   *Ibid.*

94   *Ibid.*

95   *Incentives in the New Industrial Order*, p 81.

96   *The Neglect of Science*, p 15.

97   Cp. Royal Commission on the Depression of Trade and Industry, *Second Report, Minutes of Evidence and Appendix*, Part I, p 29, no. 1628. See, also, p 145, no. 4324, and p 252, no. 6786.

98   *Ibid.*, p 21, no. 1402.

99   See, for example, Cardwell, *op. cit.*, p 104.

100 *Ibid.*, p 135.

101 Cited in Cardwell, *op. cit.*, p 104.

102 Board of Education, Report for 1908–9. Quoted in Cardwell, *op. cit.*, p 167.

103 Cardwell, *op. cit.*, p 168.

104 *Ibid.*, p 168.

105 H.J.Habakkuk, *American and British Technology in the Nineteenth Century* (Cambridge, Cambridge University Press, 1962). See, for example, p 199.

106 The point about Anglo-American wage differentials and technological advance should not be confused with some of the arguments that have been advanced concerning the *decline* in real wages which appeared to have occurred between the late 'nineties and the outbreak of the war. Thus, it has been alleged that in Britain this decline removed an important impetus to mechanization. But surely the truth of the matter is that the decline – or what Professor Phelps Brown has called the 'climacteric' of the eighteen-nineties – was international in scope, afflicting those economies that enjoyed a high rate of technical progress as well as those that did not. (Cf. E.H.Phelps Brown and S.J.Handfield-Jones, 'The Climacteric of the 1890's: A Study in the Expanding Economy', *Oxford Economic Papers*, Vol. 4, October 1952, p 285.)

107 Cp. E.Rothbarth, *op. cit.*, pp 385–6. For a rigorous statement of the problem of factor price relationships and technological advance, see W.E.G.Salter, *op. cit.*, pp 66–73.

108 *Op. cit.*, p 302.

ens, *op. cit.*, pp 50–1.

Hutchison, *The Decline and Fall of British Capitalism* rk, Scribner, 1950), p 71.

lications and conclusions that I have drawn from such ions are admittedly open to question. However, my belief of the important implications is that suggested above has rengthened by discussions with Mr George Aitken, research of the Amalgamated Engineering Union, and Mr Rodney Dobson, formerly research officer of the National Union of Tailors and Garment Workers. (See, also, Barbara Wootton, *The Social Foundations of Wages Policy* [London, Allen and Unwin, 1955], especially pp 40, 48, 50, 68–70, and 128–9.)

112 Mosely Industrial Commission to the USA, *op. cit.*, p 7.

113 L. Rostas, *op. cit.*, p 66 (Italics added.)

CHAPTER 5

1 E. A. Pratt, *op. cit.*, pp 130 and 138.

2 *Ibid.*, p 174.

3 *Industrial Efficiency*, pp 78 and 108.

4 *Report of the Tariff Commission* (London, King), Vol. 2, *The Textile Trades*, Part 1 (1905), para. 88. See, also, Vol. 2, Part 1, para. 402, and Vol. 1, *The Iron and Steel Trades* (1904), para. 747.

5 Royal Commission on Labour, *Answers to Schedules of Questions*, Group 'C' [Cd. 6795–ix] 1892, p 567.

6 Royal Commission on Labour, *Answers to Schedules of Questions*, Group 'A' [Cd. 6795–vii] 1892, p 248.

7 Royal Commission on the Poor Laws and Relief of Distress, Appendix Vol. IX, *Minutes of Evidence* [Cd. 5068] 1910, p 91, nos. 91, 207–8.

8 'A generation ago it was assumed, as a matter of course, by almost every educated person, that it was a cardinal tenet of Trade Unionism to oppose machinery and the introduction of improved processes of manufacture . . . Nowadays [*c.* 1897] we hear no such complaints.' (S. and B. Webb, *Industrial Democracy*, second edition [London, Longmans, 1919], pp 392–3.)

9 Mosely Industrial Commission to the USA, *op. cit.*, p 16.

10 Royal Commission on Labour, *Minutes of Evidence*, Vol. III [Cd. 6894–ix] 1893, p 260, no. 27,349.

11 *Ibid.*, p 353, nos. 29,400–2.

12 *Ibid.*, Vol. II [Cd. 6795–vi] 1893, p 204, nos. 16,123–4.

13 Mosely Industrial Commission to the USA, *op. cit.*, pp 67, 74, 173, 202 and 213.

14 S. and B. Webb, *Industrial Democracy*, second edition, p 395. 'Among

the thousand-and-one rules of existing Trade Unions we have discovered only one survival of the old irreconcilable prohibition, and that in a tiny local industry, which is rapidly fading away. The Operative Pearl Button and Stud Workers' Protection Society, established at Birmingham in 1843, and numbering about 500 members, enjoys the distinction of being, so far as we are aware, the only British Trade Union which still prohibits working by machinery. Its latest [1887] "Rules and Regulations" declare that "the system of centering by the engine be annihilated 'in toto', and any member countenancing the system direct or indirect shall be subject to a fine of two pounds. Any member of the Society working at the trade by means of mill-power either direct or indirect, shall be subject to a fine of five pounds." ' (*Ibid.*)

15 P 146.
16 Royal Commission on Labour, *Answers to Schedules of Questions*, Group 'C', p 151.
17 Royal Commission on Labour, *Minutes of Evidence Taken Before Group 'C'*, Vol. II [Cd. 6795–vi] 1893, p 228, nos. 16,687–8.
18 *Report of Proceedings at the Forty-Sixth Annual Trades Union Congress*, 1913, p 91.
19 Board of Trade (Labour Department), *Report on Strikes and Lock-outs in the UK in 1902* [Cd. 1623] 1903, pp 94–5.
20 *Report on Strikes and Lock-outs in the UK in 1913* [Cd. 7658] 1914, pp 148–53. Writing of the turn of the century, the Webbs observed that 'The latest case in which a union ordered a strike simply against the introduction of machinery into a hand industry is, so far as we know, that of the Liverpool Packing Case Makers' Society in 1886. The strike failed, and the men have since worked amicably with the machine, . . .' (*Industrial Democracy*, p 395, footnote.)
21 Royal Commission on Labour, *Minutes of Evidence*, Vol. I [Cd. 6708–vi] 1892, p 98, no. 2511, and Vol. II [Cd. 6795–vi] 1893, p 142, nos. 14,898–9.
22 Shadwell, *Industrial Efficiency*, p 560. But a generous measure of such 'help', in so far as the *rank and file* were concerned, was doubtless the exception rather than the rule.
23 Royal Commission on the Depression of Trade and Industry, *Second Report*, Minutes of Evidence and Appendix, Part I, p 176, no. 5,142.
24 *Report of Proceedings of the Fortieth Annual Trades Union Congress*, 1907, p 47.
25 'As regards the restriction of output, there seems to have been in certain quarters a belief that there is only a certain amount of work to be done, and that it is necessary that this work should be spread over the largest number of workmen possible.' (*Report of the Departmental Committee . . . [on] the Engineering Trades After the War*, p 13.)

26 G.D.H.Cole was of a contrary opinion. 'There is . . . no evidence at all of [the] existence [of ca' canny] in any widespread form. It has been adopted occasionally for particular purposes . . .' (*The Payment of Wages*, rev. ed., 1928, p 23.)

27 *Report of the Departmental Committee Appointed by the Board of Trade to Consider the Position of the Shipping and Shipbuilding Industries After the War* [Cd. 9092] 1918, p 27. See, also, D.L.Burn, *The Economic History of Steelmaking 1867–1939*, p 147.

28 P 28. On the other hand, at a later date the Committee on Industry and Trade reported in its *Survey of the Metal Industries* (1928) that 'Complaints regarding labour restriction of output [in the iron and steel industry] are not of serious importance . . .' (p 39)

29 *Report of the Departmental Committee . . . [on] the Iron and Steel Trades After the War*, p 28.

30 *Report of the Departmental Committee . . . [on] the Engineering Trades After the War*, p 13.

31 See E.A.Pratt, *op. cit.*, p 179, and the *Report of the Departmental Committee . . . [on] the Shipping and Shipbuilding Industries After the War*, p 24.

32 'There are very few trade unions connected with boot and shoe manufacture in which any attempt is made to specify the amount of work a man shall do in a given period . . . At the same time, there is a clear understanding that a man shall not do more than a certain quantity.' (E.A.Pratt, *op. cit.*, p 65.) For the glass industry, see the *Report of the Tariff Commission*, Vol. 6, paras. 58–9, 73–4, and for typesetting, see E.A.Pratt, *op. cit.*, p 65. As regards coal-mining, Lord Askwith records the following allegation: 'In the collieries the restriction is exercised indirectly. If a miner exceeds a certain output per day, varying from four to seven tons, he finds himself delayed by the "shunt" men, who cut down his supply of tubs and props.' (*Industrial Problems and Disputes* [London, Murray, 1920], p 302. See, also, the Minutes of Evidence taken before the Royal Commission on Trade Disputes and Trade Combinations [Cd. 2826] 1906, p 63, no. 1002.)

33 *Op. cit.*, p 28. See, also, a letter to the editor of *The Economist*, 26 December 1908, p 1242.

34 *The Payment of Wages*, rev. ed. (1928), pp 23–4.

35 Lord Askwith, *op. cit.*, p 303.

36 Reprinted in J.R.Commons (ed.), *Trade Unionism and Labor Problems* (1905 ed.), p 301.

37 *Op. cit.*, pp 26–7.

38 Cf. Amalgamated Engineers' *Monthly Journal*, September 1900, p 18; February 1901, p 3; January 1902, p 73; November 1902, p 94; and July 1904, p 2.

39 Quoted in G.D.H.Cole, *The Payment of Wages*, 1918 ed., p 129. This is substantially the same as one of the clauses of the agreement between the same two parties that was drafted in 1899. (See the Minutes of Evidence taken before the Royal Commission on Trade Disputes and Trade Combinations, Appendices [Cd. 2826] 1906, p 86.)

40 *Op. cit.*, p 59.

41 P 22.

42 *The Payment of Wages*, rev. ed. (1928), p 24. In a footnote on the same page Cole wrote that there are 'practically' no trade union rules which regulate output per unit of time. His earlier observations on the matter had left no room for exceptions.

43 P 27.

44 *The Payment of Wages* (1918 ed.), p 122.

45 From an agreement between the Master Printers' and Allied Trades' Association and the London Society of Compositors, as recorded in the Board of Trade's *Report on Standard Piece Rates of Wages and Sliding-Scales in the United Kingdom* [Cd. 144] 1900, p 236.

46 Board of Trade (Labour Dept.), *Report on Strikes and Lock-outs in the UK in 1908* [Cd. 4680] 1909, pp 114–7.

47 For example, [Cd. 3711] 1907, pp 90–3. See, also, the *Eighth Report of the Board of Trade of Proceedings under the Conciliation (Trades Disputes) Act, 1896* (96), 1911.

48 See J.Ashford, 'Light Lathes and Screw Machines', *The Engineer*, March 1901, p 249.

49 In 1906, the Engineering Employers' Federation claimed that 'out of 46 ["Federated"] districts employing [turret] lathes, there were only seven where these lathes are manned by skilled men. The whole of the other 39 districts are manned by handymen'. (The Amalgamated Engineers' *Report and Monthly Record*, September 1906, p 30.)

50 '[It] is the practice in many establishments to employ boys to attend simple tools, and keep them at work year in and year out on exactly the same set of operations . . .' (*The Engineer*, 9 March 1900, p 256.) See, also, the Amalgamated Engineers' *Report and Monthly Record*, February 1910, p 18 (Report of Organizing District Delegate No 3); R.H.Tawney, 'The Economics of Boy Labour', *Economic Journal*, Vol. 19, December 1909, p 535; and the Royal Commission on the Poor Laws and Relief of Distress, Appendix Vol. VIII, *Minutes of Evidence* [Cd. 5066] 1910, p 764, no 82.)

51 C.Jackson, in his report on boy labour for the Poor Law Commission, wrote that information received from engineering employers did not indicate that there had been any decrease in the proportion of unskilled to skilled workers in the engineering trades. What was indicated, however, according to Jackson, was an increase in the relative

importance of the semi-skilled. (Royal Commission on the Poor Laws and Relief of Distress, Appendix Vol. XX, *Report by C.Jackson on Boy Labour* [Cd. 4632] 1909, p 132.)

52 The displacement of skilled workers in engineering shops was of course carried to much more extreme lengths during the war. Unskilled workers who entered the wartime munitions industry were eventually put to work on almost every type of machine tool. Indeed, with division of labour often being pushed to a technical maximum, unskilled workers were engaged in tasks hitherto believed to have been impossible of execution without the services of highly skilled men. (See *The History of the Ministry of Munitions*, Vol. IV, parts 1 and 4.)

53 See the Factory Report for 1902 [Cd. 1610] 1903, p 126; D. Pollock, *The Shipbuilding Industry* (London, Methuen, 1950), p 91; and the Royal Commission on the Poor Laws and Relief of Distress, Appendix Vol. VIII, *Minutes of Evidence*, no. 85,727.

54 Cf. Royal Commission on Labour, *Answers to Schedules of Questions*, Group 'C', p 153.

55 After the protracted struggle of 1897 – ostensibly precipitated by the demand of the London engineers for an eight-hour day, but actually set in motion by the 'manning of machines' question – an agreement was signed (1898) between the Engineering Employers' Federation and the Allied Engineering Trades. Among other things, the agreement provided that 'Employers are responsible for the work turned out by their machine tools, and shall have full discretion to appoint the men they consider best adapted to the various operations carried on in their workshops'. This agreement was superseded in 1907 by the 'Terms of Agreement' between the Engineering Employers' Federation, and the Amalgamated Society of Engineers, the Steam Engine Makers' Society and the United Machine Workers Association. (A number of other unions with memberships in the engineering trades acceded to the Terms of Agreement later on.) Clause 7 ('Selection, Training and Employment of Operatives and Manning of Machine Tools') reproduced, *verbatim*, the stipulation of the 1898 settlement relating to the employers' right to 'select, train, and employ . . .' and then went on to specify, in language almost identical to that used in the 1898 document, that 'Employers, in view of the necessity of obtaining the most economic production whether by skilled or unskilled workmen, have full discretion to appoint the men they consider suitable to work all their machine tools and to determine the conditions under which they shall be worked'. In 1912, the unions attempted to have Clause 7 rescinded, or at least modified, but the employers would have none of it. (Cf. Amalgamated Engineers' *Report and Monthly Record*, March 1912, pp 19 ff. and June 1912, pp 12 ff.) Finally, in December 1913, the ASE

notified the employers that it did not wish to renew the 1907 Terms of Agreement and the latter simply expired in March 1914. (Amalgamated Engineers' *Monthly Journal and Report*, June 1914, p 15.)

56 Amalgamated Engineers' *Monthly Journal*, February 1901, p 63.

57 Amalgamated Engineers' *Monthly Journal*, September 1902, p 77.

58 Amalgamated Engineers' *Monthly Journal*, June 1912, p 25.

59 Amalgamated Engineers' *Monthly Journal and Report*, August 1913, p 45.

60 Amalgamated Engineers' *Monthly Journal*, February 1902, p 71.

61 See J. B. Jefferys, *The Story of the Engineers* (London, Lawrence and Wishart, 1945), p 166.

62 See Jefferys, *op. cit.*, *loc. cit.*, and S. and B. Webb, *The History of Trade Unionism* (London, Longmans, 1920), p 486.

63 See W. Mosses, *op. cit.*, p 232.

64 See, for example, the *Report on Strikes and Lock-outs in the UK in 1904* [Cd. 2631] 1905, pp 88–91; and the Reports of the Proceedings of the 1911 (p 242), 1912 (p 239), and 1913 (p 86) Trades Union Congresses.

65 When asked by the Labour Commission what their attitude to the introduction of labour-saving machinery was, the Scottish Typographical Association (Airdrie and Coatbridge) replied that 'so far as practicable these [machines should] be worked by men who served the regular term of apprenticeship'. (Royal Commission on Labour, *Answers to Schedules of Questions*, Group 'C', p 162.)

66 The 1898 agreement between the Linotype Users' Association and the Typographical Association (the union of the provincial compositors) contained the following provision:

'3 All skilled operators shall be members of the Typographical Association, and, on the introduction of composing machines into any office, preference shall, as far as possible, be given to the members of the companionship into which they are introduced.' (Quoted in Board of Trade [Labour Dept.], *Report on Collective Agreements between Employers and Workpeople in the UK* [Cd. 5366] 1910, p 301.)

The 1909 (amended) agreement between the Master Printers' and Allied Trades' Association, and the London Society of Compositors contained this clause:

'(*a*) *News Scale – Daily Papers.*

Members of the Companionship into which machines are introduced . . . shall be given facilities to learn them in their own time . . . and when learners have reached an output of 4,000 ens in a test hour, . . . preference shall be given to such qualified learners, . . .' (*Ibid.*, p 295.)

67 The provision for indentured apprenticeship was not quite moribund. It was still to be found in many collective agreements and arbitration

awards of the period. The following agreements and awards – the list is not exhaustive – all contained regulations to the effect that apprentices were to be legally bound: Birmingham bricklayers and their employers (1910); the Manchester Operative Masons and the Manchester Building Trades' Employers Association (1909); the Associated Society of Carpenters and Joiners, and the Liverpool Master Builders' Association (1908); the National Association of Operative Plasterers and two federations of building trades employers (1904); the United Society of Boilermakers and Iron and Steel Shipbuilders, and the Shipbuilding Employers' Federation (1901); the Liverpool coopers and their employers (1908); and the cabinet makers and furnishing trades unions of Liverpool, and two employers' associations of the same city (1908). (See Board of Trade [Labour Dept.], *Report on Collective Agreements Between Employers and Workpeople in the UK*, and the Minutes of Evidence taken before the Royal Commission on Trade Disputes and Trade Combinations, p 81.)

However, in many cases the indenture provision, although not entirely a dead letter, did not prevent apprentices from becoming more numerous than considered desirable by the unions, as witness the constant complaints on this score by shipyard and boilershop workers. Nor, in several instances, did a mere agreement provide an impregnable barrier against the entry of entirely unapprenticed boy labour.

68 '[The] time-honoured distinction between (1) learners or apprentices who are employed, not for their immediate commercial utility, but in order to maintain at a future date the supply of adult workmen in the industry (e.g. apprentice masons, joiners, fitters, etc.); and (2) boys who are not being taught any [skilled] occupations with a view to their practising it as men, but who are employed, to quote the words of an employer, "solely for their immediate commercial utility" upon some simple operation, and who, to distinguish them from boy learners may be called boy labourers . . . has for many years been undergoing a gradual process of obliteration . . .' (R.H. Tawney, *op. cit.*, pp 518–9. See, also, the Royal Commission on the Poor Laws and Relief of Distress, Appendix Vol. IX, *Minutes of Evidence*, no. 94,039; and the LCC Education Committee, *Report of the Section . . . Appointed to Consider the Question of Apprenticeship* [No. 925, 1909], p 1.) However, this was not universally the case. In some of those industries which had not fallen victim to mechanization and in which, in addition, subdivision of process had not been pushed very far, the traditional 'all-round' apprentice training, although not always accepted wholeheartedly by employers, still persisted. Thus, we find in an arbitration award made in the London bookbinding trade in 1903, the provision that 'apprentices shall be trained not merely in

a sub-section but in a branch' of the trade. (Board of Trade [Labour Dept.], *Report on Collective Agreements between Employers and Workpeople in the UK*, p 310.)

Some idea of how the apprenticeship system (indentured and un-indentured) was faring in the British industry of seventy and eighty years ago may be gleaned from the Royal Commission on Labour, *Answers to Schedules of Questions*, Group 'A', pp 234 ff., and Group 'C', pp 114 ff. and pp 775 ff.; and the Royal Commission on the Poor Laws and Relief of Distress, Appendix Vol. XX, *Report by C. Jackson on Boy Labour*.

69 Cf. the Board of Trade (Labour Dept.), *Report on Collective Agreements between Employers and Workpeople in the UK*; the Reports on Strikes and Lock-outs; the Reports on Conciliation and Arbitration Boards for 1900 (p 82) and for 1903 (p 102); and the Amalgamated Engineers' *Report and Monthly Record*, April 1905, p 8 (Organizing District Delegate No. 2, Liverpool), October 1908, p 21 (ODD No. 7, Stratford), and January 1910, p 28 (ODD No. 5, Sheffield).

70 S. and B. Webb, *Industrial Democracy*, pp 408–9.

71 Quoted in D. C. Cummings, *A Historical Survey of the Boiler Makers' and Iron and Steel Ship Builders' Society* (Newcastle-on-Tyne, 1905), p 191.

72 See S. and B. Webb, *Industrial Democracy*, pp 395–6.

73 Amalgamated Engineers' *Monthly Journal*, June 1902, p 73 (Report of Organizing District Delegate No. 1, Glasgow).

74 *Report of the Proceedings of the Fortieth Annual Trades Union Congress*, 1907, p 47.

75 *Industrial Democracy*, p 411.

76 'In Lancashire it quickly becomes a grievance in the Cotton Trade Unions, if any one employer or any one district falls behind the rest ... The old-fashioned master spinners, with slow-going family concerns, complain bitterly of the harshness with which the Trade Union officials refuse to make any allowance for their relatively imperfect machinery, and even insist ... on their paying positively a higher piece-work rate if they do not work their mills as efficiently as their best-equipped competitors. Thus, the Amalgamated Association of Operative Cotton-spinners, instead of obstructing new machinery, actually penalises the employer who fails to introduce it.' (S. and B. Webb, *Industrial Democracy*, p 413. For similar observations, see J. W. F. Rowe, *Wages in Practice and Theory* [London, Routledge, 1928], p 165.)

77 S. and B. Webb, *Industrial Democracy*, pp 425–6.

78 *Ibid.*, p 425.

79 *Ibid.*, p 424. Nevertheless, the unions complained that the 'rapid

crease of this class of spinning [i.e., ring-spinning] is preventing the extension of mule spinning'. (*Ibid.*, p 427.) Eventually, one of the unions in the industry met the situation by admitting the ring-spinners to membership. (*Ibid.*, p 424, footnote.)

80 *Op. cit.*, p 136.
81 *Epilogue*, Vol. 1, *1895–1905* (London, Unwin, 1929), p 214.
82 Quoted in the Amalgamated Engineers' *Monthly Journal*, October 1910, p 36.
83 *Ibid.*
84 *Ibid.*
85 *Ibid.*

APPENDICES TO CHAPTER 5

A

1 See, for example, the *Monthly Journal* for July 1901, p 3.
2 *Report of Proceedings of the Fortieth Annual Trades Union Congress*, 1907, p 177.
3 *Report of Proceedings of the Forty-Third Annual Trades Union Congress*, 1910, p 194.
4 'Under the speed and feed system the workmen were dodged, dogged and clocked by supervisors; and it was very disagreeable, indeed, to work under.' (*Ibid.*) 'The aggravation . . . to a man who is told to increase the speed of his machine tool, when he knows he is getting the best result from the one he is using, is very great.' (Amalgamated Engineers' *Monthly Journal*, October 1910, p 37.)
5 'The British workman takes a pride in turning out his best, but the feed and speed system now so largely adopted effectually prevents any delight being taken in making good work, any suggestion regarding finish being generally met with "Do as you are told; we don't pay you to think." ' (Amalgamated Engineers' *Monthly Journal*, July 1901, p 3 ['Monthly Preface'].)
6 '[The control of the feed and speed men] is frequently resented, and naturally so. Their duties are to determine the cuts, feeds and speeds for the work of each machine in the shop, so removing initiative, and to that extent responsibility, from the [machine-tool operator]. It is, to say the least, a curious and anomalous relation, and the inevitable result of the general adoption of such a system must be to degrade the present race of craftsmen into machine minders.' (From 'Roughing Tools for Lathe Work', *English Mechanic and World of Science*, 24 June 1910, and quoted in the Amalgamated Engineers' *Monthly Journal*, October 1910, p 36.)
7 See the motion introduced against the feed and speed system at the

1910 Trades Union Congress. (*Report of Proceedings of the Forty-Third Annual Trades Union Congress*, p 194.)

8   Here, however, is a contrary opinion, taken from the summary of the evidence given by a trade union witness to the TUC Joint Committee on the Premium Bonus System: '[The witness] had been under the feed and speed system, against which he had little complaint to make. One feed and speed overseer had five or six workshops to overlook, and in many cases his supervision was only nominal.' (*Report of the TUC Joint Committee on the Premium Bonus System*, 1910, p 34.)

9   *Report of Proceedings of the Fortieth Annual TUC*, p 177.

10 See the Amalgamated Engineers' *Monthly Journal*, September 1902, pp 71–3.

11 J.B.Jefferys, *op. cit.*, p 155.

12 See the Engineering and Allied Employers' National Federation, *Decisions of Central Conference, 1898–1925*, Reference Nos. 122, 681, 714, 942, 950, 1,034, 1,035, 1,244, 1,246, 1,397, 1,398 (2), 1,415, 1,436 and 1,495.

13 See the *Report of the TUC Joint Committee on the Premium Bonus System*, 1910.

14 *Ibid.*, pp 73–4.

15 'This month we publish an article on premium bonus. This is a question of vital importance to our members. It has added to the worry and uncertainty of workshop life. Those who believe that it was introduced to benefit the workers must by this time realise that they were either deceived or misinformed.' (Amalgamated Engineers' *Monthly Journal*, August 1911, p 4.)

16 One of the chief complaints voiced by trade unionists in regard to the setting of standard times was that rate-fixers were prone to err on the side of underestimation. Numerous such allegations appear in the evidence heard by the TUC's Joint Committee on Premium Bonus. Sometimes it was maintained that the error was deliberate. (See, for example, the Amalgamated Engineers' *Monthly Journal*, June 1904, p 16; November 1904, p 90; December 1904, p 71.) Whatever may be said about intent, it is doubtless true that basis-time determination was, during the early years of the system, often a rather crude, hit-and-miss affair. Even an employer (Sir Benjamin Browne, the shipbuilder) had complained of the 'clumsy' methods of fixing times (and prices) which, he believed, had brought such systems of payment by results 'into ill repute'. (Quoted in the Amalgamated Engineers' *Monthly Journal*, April 1901, p 6.)

17 Royal Commission on Labour, *Minutes of Evidence taken before Group 'A'*, Vol. III [Cd. 6894–vii] 1893, p 166, no 22,943. See, also,

E. H. Phelps Brown, *The Growth of British Industrial Relations* (London, Macmillan, 1959), p 56.

B

1 One category of dispute that some might be inclined to group with those listed in the Tables has been omitted. This was the demarcation dispute – or, in the jargon of the Labour Department, the dispute 'between classes of workpeople' – which was a particularly common occurrence in the engineering and shipbuilding trades. Platers, riveters, and caulkers frequently battled with shipwrights and engineers over the 'right' to a certain process or type of work. Sometimes these disputes were provoked by the introduction of a new machine, but this was not always the case. (Demarcation disputes were, typically, disputes between groups of skilled workers, rather than disputes over the employment of unskilled workers.) Thus, if demarcation disputes had been included in the Tables, the latter would have covered a great deal of industrial strife which did not arise out of attempts to introduce some cost-reducing change in technique or redeployment of the labour force, and the like.

CHAPTER 6

1 As to qualitative differences and utilization costs, in 1907–9, 2·09 tons of coal were used to produce a ton of pig-iron in Britain as against 1·74 tons in the United States. (Taussig, *op. cit.*, p 105.) For data and observations on extraction costs in the two countries, see the *Report of the Departmental Committee Appointed by the Board of Trade to Consider the Position of the Coal Trade After the War* [Cd. 9093] 1918, p 8.

2 Frankel, *op. cit.*, pp 38–9; and W. Duane Evans, *op. cit.*, p 117.

3 Although the frontier exerted its influence upon the *use* of capital in the United States, still, the rate of capital formation in that country was much greater than it was in Britain. (See page 127, below.)

4 F. J. Turner, *The Frontier in American History* (New York, Holt, 1920), especially pp 37–8. See, also, Frankel, *op. cit.*, *loc. cit.*, and Evans, *op. cit.*, *loc. cit.*

5 *Op. cit.*

6 *Op. cit.*

7 Cp. Fabricant, *op. cit.*, pp 47–9.

8 *Ibid.*, p 46.

9 See pp 138–140, below.

10 In 1871, the population of the United Kingdom was 31·6 million and that of the United States 40·9 million.

11 Cf. E. Rothbarth, *op. cit.*, pp 383–4.

12 Rostas, *op. cit.*, p 61, footnote. We might point out again that one of the members of the Commission – and one who had apparently been infected with considerable enthusiasm for what he saw of American practice – was (the then) Mr Joseph Whitworth. Whitworth had by this time already made his mark on British engineering practice. (See, also, Rothbarth, *op. cit.*, *loc. cit.*, and p 12, above.)

13 Rostas, *op. cit.*, pp 58–9. See, also, S. Dell, 'Economic Integration and the American Example', *Economic Journal*, Vol. 69, March 1959, pp 40–1; Frankel, *op. cit.*, p 69; and Fabricant, *op. cit.*, pp 40–1.

14 On the other hand, as has already been pointed out, there were many branches of the engineering trades that were eminently suited for standardized repetition work, given the appropriate reorganization of productive processes and the installation of the necessary machines.

15 For another critique of the export argument, see Frankel, *op. cit.*, pp 70, 72–3, 76.

16 Cf. Rothbarth, *op. cit.*, p 386.

17 'The British dependence on the varied demands of numerous foreign markets explains in some degree the reluctance of British industry to adopt the policies of standardization and specialization which, even before 1914, were enabling foreign manufacturers, particularly Americans, to lower their costs . . . Whether this provides a complete explanation of the contrast is debatable. Some critics believed that British industry was suffering from inertia and complacency, penalties of its early start.' (G. C. Allen, *British Industries and Their Organization*, p 12.)

18 *New York Industrial Exhibition: Special Report of Mr George Wallis*, Parliamentary Papers, 1854, Vol. XXXV, p 14; quoted in D. L. Burn, 'The Genesis of American Engineering Competition, 1850–1870', *Economic History*, Vol. 2, January 1931, p 307.

19 D. J. Coppock, *op. cit.*, p 24.

20 Cf. Rostas, *op. cit.*, pp 55–6.

21 G. Terborgh, *Technological Stagnation in Great Britain* (Chicago, Machinery and Allied Products Institute, 1948); cited in Rostas, *op. cit.*, p 56.

22 The Committee added that 'In some districts, however (*particularly those where the development of industry was more recent*), the scale of production was on the whole larger and the organization and plant more up-to-date than in the older districts'. (*Survey of the Metal Industries*, pp 8–9 [italics added].)

23 'The patchwork development of British [iron and steel] works indicated a lack of appreciation of the fundamental effect on unit direct costs derived from large-scale outlay, even if this involved a new start. The industry would not accept the dictum that economic by-gones are

by-gones, yet it was no use trying to carry over small industrial units into the mass production machine. British costs of production were influenced by the past history of the industry and there was much less readiness compared, for example, with the USA, to take up new methods and processes, or to plan for future demand.' (Burnham and Hoskins, *op. cit.*, p 269.)

24 F. R. Jervis, 'The Handicap of Britain's Early Start', *Manchester School of Social and Economic Studies*, Vol. 15, January 1947, p 120.

25 New York, Viking, 1942 (p 130, 'The Case of England').

26 M. Frankel, 'Obsolescence and Technological Change in a Maturing Economy', *American Economic Review*, Vol. 45, June 1955, pp 296–319.

27 *Ibid.*, p 297.

28 *Ibid.*, pp 313–4.

29 For a general statement of the alleged advantages of a later start, see, also, W. A. Lewis, *The Theory of Economic Growth* (London, Allen & Unwin, 1955), pp 345–6.

30 *National Income and Outlay* (London, Macmillan, 1937), p 272.

31 *Ibid.*

32 Cp. W. A. Lewis, *The Theory of Economic Growth*, pp 299–301; and M. Frankel, *British and American Manufacturing Productivity*, p 88.

33 Cf. Marshall, *Principles of Economics*, 8th ed., p 266.

34 *Ibid.*

35 Cp. D. J. Coppock, *op. cit.*, pp 23, 26–30.

36 See A. E. Musson, 'The Great Depression in Britain, 1873–96: A Reappraisal', *Journal of Economic History*, Vol. 19, June 1959, p 210; and Brinley Thomas, *Migration and Economic Growth* (Cambridge, Cambridge University Press, 1954), pp 229–30.

37 See J. Steindl, *Small and Big Business. Economic Problems of the Size of Firms* (New York, Oxford University Press, 1945) pp 63–5.

38 See W. A. Lewis, *Overhead Costs. Some Essays in Economic Analysis* (London, Allen & Unwin, 1949), pp 157–9. Lewis cites the Mogul Steamship Company case, 1892, as 'the decisive watershed'. (*Ibid.*, p 158.)

39 J. H. Clapham, *op. cit.*, Vol. 2, pp 149–50.

40 *Ibid.*, Vol. 3, pp 304–5. See, also, E. H. Phelps Brown, *The Growth of British Industrial Relations*, pp 137–41.

41 J. H. Clapham, *op. cit.*, Vol. 3, p 182. Protectionists, especially those of a more chauvinistic hue, might argue that the case in question was not altogether grist to the free trader's mill, for the revolution in the British boot and shoe trade was not due solely to British initiative. An extra-territorial foray of American capital and enterprise played its part, too. As Professor Clapham himself pointed out, 'America had a grip on the British [shoe] industry ... through its machinery – a grip which dated

from about 1900. By 1913 some 80 per cent of the manufacturing firms, it is said, were clients for many important machines of American origin to a company which though half English in capital and management had its centre of will-power . . . in the United States.' (*Ibid.*, pp 182–3.) Of course, a good economic liberal would retort that this case provides an excellent support for the free-trade position. After all, is not the international movement of entrepreneurship to be applauded, and if free trade conduced to such movement, then free trade must be accounted a 'good thing'! Still, when one recalls that the entrepreneurship in question sprang from what was to be a classic textbook example (in the United States) of monopoly control, the shoe machinery case leaves something to be desired – at least from the point of view of the liberal position.

42 Joseph Chamberlain, *Imperial Union and Tariff Reform, Speeches Delivered from 15 May to 4 November 1903* (London, Grant Richards, 1903), p 141.

43 *Ibid.*

44 W. A. S. Hewins, *Trade in the Balance* (London, Philip Allan, 1924), p 71.

45 *Ibid.*, p 68.

46 *Ibid.*, p 86.

47 *Ibid.*, p 74.

48 *Ibid.*, p 35.

49 *Ibid.*, p 24.

CHAPTER 7

1 *Op. cit.*

Bibliography

Lord Aberconway, *The Basic Industries of Great Britain*, London, Benn, 1927.

G.C.Allen, *British Industries and their Organisation*, 3rd ed., London, Longmans, 1951.

——, *The Industrial Development of Birmingham and the Black Country 1860–1927*, London, Allen & Unwin, 1929.

Amalgamated Engineers' *Monthly Journal*.

—— *Monthly Journal and Report*.

—— *Monthly Record*.

—— *Report and Monthly Record*.

E.C.Amos, 'Portable Pneumatic Tools', *The Engineer*, 30 March 1900.

——, 'Workshop Practice at the Beginning of the Twentieth Century', *The Engineer*, 15 March, 1901.

W.Arnold, 'The Engineer and the Economical Development of Manufactories', *The Engineer*, 31 August 1900.

J.Ashford, 'Light Lathes and Screw Machines', *The Engineer*, March 1901.

W.J.Ashley, *British Industries. A Series of General Reviews for Business Men and Students*, London, Longmans, 1907.

Lord Askwith, *Industrial Problems and Disputes*, London, Murray, 1920.

G.E.Barnett, 'The Introduction of the Linotype', in J.R.Commons (ed.), *Trade Unionism and Labor Problems* (Boston, Ginn, 1905), pp 250–73.

Messrs Barr and Stroud, *Notes on the Premium System of Wage-Earning*, 1902.

J.Wolfe Barry, 'Standardisation in British Engineering Practice', *The Mechanical Engineer*, 1 September 1906, pp 285–8.

H.L.Beales, 'The "Basic" Industries of England, 1850–1914', *Economic History Review*, Vol. 5, April 1935, pp 99–112.

——, 'The "Great Depression" in Industry and Trade', *Economic History Review*, Vol. 5, October 1934, pp 65–75.

M.Beer, *A History of British Socialism*, London, Allen & Unwin, 1948.

J.M.Blair, 'Technology and Size', *American Economic Review*, Vol. 38, May 1948, pp 121–52.

184

H. I. Brackenbury, 'High-Speed Tools and Machines to Fit Them', *Proceedings* of the Institution of Mechanical Engineers, 1910, pp 929–55; 986–1026.

—— 'Modern Machinery and Its Future Development', *The Engineer*, 23 August 1907.

R. A. Bray, *Boy Labour and Apprenticeship*, London, Constable, 1911.

British Standards Institution, *Fifty Years of British Standards*, London, 1951.

E. H. Phelps Brown, *The Growth of British Industrial Relations*, London, Macmillan, 1959.

E. H. Phelps Brown and S. J. Handfield-Jones, 'The Climacteric of the 1890's: A Study in the Expanding Economy', *Oxford Economic Papers*, Vol. 4, October 1952, pp 266–307.

E. H. Phelps Brown and B. Weber, 'Accumulation, Productivity and Distribution in the British Economy, 1870–1938', *Economic Journal*, Vol. 63, June 1953, pp 263–88.

D. L. Burn, *The Economic History of Steelmaking 1867–1939*, Cambridge, Cambridge University Press, 1940.

——, 'The Genesis of American Engineering Competition, 1850–1870', *Economic History*, Vol. 2, January 1931, pp 292–311.

T. H. Burnham and G. O. Hoskins, *Iron and Steel in Britain 1870–1930*, London, Allen & Unwin, 1943.

F. G. Burton, *The Commercial Management of Engineering Works*, 2nd ed., Manchester, The Scientific Publishing Co., 1905.

E. Cadbury, 'Some Principles of Industrial Organisation. The Case For and Against Scientific Management', *The Sociological Review*, Vol. 7, April 1914, pp 99–125, 266–9, and 315–31.

A. K. Cairncross, *Home and Foreign Investment 1870–1913*, Cambridge, Cambridge University Press, 1953.

D. S. L. Cardwell, *The Organization of Science in England*, London, Heinemann, 1957.

H. N. Casson, *Factory Efficiency. How to Increase Output, Wages, Dividends and Good-will*, 2nd ed., London, The Efficiency Magazine, 1918.

Joseph Chamberlain, *Imperial Union and Tariff Reform. Speeches Delivered from 15 May to 4 November 1903*, London, Grant Richards, 1903.

J. H. Clapham, *An Economic History of Modern Britain*, Vol. 3, *Machines and National Rivalries (1887–1914)*, Cambridge, Cambridge University Press, 1938.

——, *The Economic Development of France and Germany 1815–1914*, 4th ed, Cambridge, Cambridge University Press, 1936.

Colin Clark, *Conditions of Economic Progress*, London, Macmillan, 1940.

——, *National Income and Outlay*, London, Macmillan, 1937.

G. D. H. Cole, *The Payment of Wages. A Study in Payment by Results under*

185

the Wage-System, London, Allen & Unwin, 1918; rev. ed., London, Allen & Unwin, 1928.

G. D. H. Cole, *The World of Labour*, London, Bell, 1919.

Committee on Industry and Trade ('Balfour Committee'), *Factors in Industrial and Commercial Efficiency*, Part I, 1927; Part II, 1928.

—— *Survey of Metal Industries*, 1928.

—— *Survey of Textile Industries*, 1928.

D. J. Coppock, 'The Climacteric of the 1890's: A Critical Note', *Manchester School of Social and Economic Studies*, Vol. 24, January 1956, pp 1–31.

E. Cressy, *Discoveries and Inventions of the Twentieth Century*, 3rd ed., London, Routledge, 1930.

——, *A Hundred Years of Mechanical Engineering*, London, Duckworth, 1937.

——, *An Outline of Industrial History*, London, Macmillan, 1934.

D. C. Cummings, *A Historical Survey of the Boiler Makers' and Iron and Steel Ship Builders' Society from August, 1834 to August, 1904*, Newcastle-on-Tyne, Robinson, 1905.

S. Dell, 'Economic Integration and the American Example', *Economic Journal*, Vol. 69, March 1959, pp 39–54.

P. Devinat, *Scientific Management in Europe*, Geneva, International Labour Office, 1927.

G. Binney Dibblee, 'The Printing Trades and the Crisis in British Industry', *Economic Journal*, Vol. 12, 1902, pp 1–12 (and reprinted in J. R. Commons, *op. cit.*, pp 289–303).

P. H. Douglas, 'An Estimate of the Growth of Capital in the United Kingdom, 1865–1909', *Journal of Economic and Business History*, Vol. 2, 1929–30, pp 659–85.

B. Drake, *Women in the Engineering Trades*, London, Fabian Research Department, 1917.

H. B. Drury, *Scientific Management: A History and Criticism*, 2nd ed., New York, Columbia, 1918.

The Economist

C. D. Edwards, 'Size of Markets, Scale of Firms and the Character of Competition', in E. A. G. Robinson (ed.), *Economic Consequences of the Size of Nations*, London, Macmillan, 1960.

E. T. Elbourne, *Factory Administration and Accounts*, London, Longmans, 1914; new ed., London, Longmans, 1919.

——, *Factory Administration and Cost Accounts*, London, Longmans, 1929.

——, 'The Technique of Industrial Administration', a series of thirty-two articles in *The Accountant*, Vol. 28 and Vol. 29, 1928.

The Engineer

Engineering and Allied Employers' National Federation, *Decisions of Central Conference 1898–1925*.

Engineering Standards Committee, *Report on British Standard Systems of Limit Gauges for Running Fits*, Publication No. 27, June 1906.

——, Reports on Work Accomplished, 1905 to 1914.

C. Erickson, *British Industrialists, Steel and Hosiery 1850–1950*, Cambridge, Cambridge University Press, 1959.

W. Duane Evans, 'Economic Development: Case Studies – Discussion', *American Economic Review*, Vol. 45, May 1955, pp 115–9.

S. Fabricant, 'Study of the Size and Efficiency of the American Economy,' in E. A. G. Robinson, *op. cit.*

A. P. M. Fleming and H. J. Brocklehurst, *A History of Engineering*, London, Black, 1925.

P. S. Florence, *The Logic of Industrial Organization*, London, Kegan Paul, 1933.

A. W. Flux, 'Industrial Productivity in Britain and the United States', *Quarterly Journal of Economics*, Vol. 48, November 1933, pp 1–38.

M. Frankel, *British and American Manufacturing Productivity*, Urbana, University of Illinois, Bureau of Economic and Business Research, 1957.

——, 'Obsolescence and Technical Change in a Maturing Economy', *American Economic Review*, Vol. 45, June 1955, pp 296–319.

E. Garcke, *The Progress of Electrical Enterprise*, London, Electrical Press, 1907.

A. Gerschenkron, 'Social Attitudes, Entrepreneurship and Economic Development', *Explorations in Entrepreneurial History*, Vol. 6, October 1953, pp 1–19.

S. C. Gilfillan, *The Sociology of Invention*, Chicago, Follet, 1935.

R. W. Goldsmith, 'Financial Structure and Economic Growth in Advanced Countries: An Experiment in Comparative Financial Morphology', in *Capital Formation and Economic Growth*, Princeton, Princeton University Press, 1955.

R. W. Goldsmith, D. S. Brady, and H. Mendershausen, *A Study of Saving in the United States*, Vol. 3, Princeton, Princeton University Press, 1955.

H. J. Habakkuk, *American and British Technology in the Nineteenth Century. The Search for Labour-Saving Inventions*, Cambridge, Cambridge University Press, 1962.

W. A. S. Hewins, 'The Influence of the New German Commercial Treaties on British Industries', *National Review*, Vol. 45, June 1905, pp 693–704.

——, *Trade in the Balance*, London, Philip Allan, 1924.

W. L. Hichens, *Some Problems of Modern Industry*, London, Nisbet, 1918.

History of the Ministry of Munitions, London, 1922.

Vol. 4, *The Supply and Control of Labour*, 1915–6.

Vol. 6, *Man Power and Dilution*.

J. A. Hobson, *The Evolution of Modern Capitalism*, rev. ed., London, Allen & Unwin, 1949.

J.A.Hobson, *Incentives in the New Industrial Order*, London, Parsons, 1922.

——, 'Scientific Management', *Sociological Review*, Vol. 6, July 1913, pp 197–212.

R.J.S.Hoffman, *Great Britain and the German Trade Rivalry 1875–1914*, Philadelphia, University of Pennsylvania Press, 1933.

W.G.Hoffmann, *British Industrial Production 1700–1950*, Oxford, Blackwell, 1955.

R.F.Hoxie, *Scientific Management and Labor*, New York, Appleton, 1918.

B.L.Hutchins, *Women in Modern Industry*, London, Bell, 1915.

K.Hutchison, *The Decline and Fall of British Capitalism*, New York, Scribner, 1950.

J.B.Jefferys, *The Story of the Engineers 1800–1945*, London, Lawrence & Wishart, 1945.

H.Jerome, *Mechanization in Industry*, New York, National Bureau of Economic Research, 1934.

F.R.J.Jervis, 'The Handicap of Britain's Early Start', *Manchester School of Social and Economic Studies*, Vol. 15, January 1947, pp 112–22.

J.Jewkes, 'Are Economies of Scale Unlimited?', in E.A.G.Robinson, *op. cit.*, pp 95–116.

——, 'Is British Industry Inefficient?', *Manchester School of Social and Economic Studies*, Vol. 14, January 1946, pp 1–16.

G.T.Jones, *Increasing Return. A Study of the Relation between the Size and Efficiency of Industries with Special Reference to the History of Selected British and American Industries 1850–1910*, Cambridge, Cambridge University Press, 1933.

S.Kuznets, 'International Differences in Capital Formation and Financing', in *Capital Formation and Economic Growth*, Princeton, Princeton University Press, 1955.

Labour and Industry in 1913 (*The Times* Series), London, Murray, 1913.

J.H.Lenfant, 'Great Britain's Capital Formation, 1865–1914', *Economica*, n.s., Vol. 18, May 1958, pp 151–68.

A.L.Levine, 'Industrial Change and Its Effects Upon Labour 1900–1914', unpublished doctoral dissertation, University of London, 1954.

W.A.Lewis, 'International Competition in Manufactures', *American Economic Review*, Vol. 47, May 1957, pp 578–87.

——, *Overhead Costs. Some Essays in Economic Analysis*, London, Allen & Unwin, 1949.

——, *The Theory of Economic Growth*, London, Allen & Unwin, 1955.

W.A.Lewis and P.J.O'Leary, 'Secular Swings in Production and Trade 1870–1913', *Manchester School of Social and Economic Studies*, Vol. 23, May 1955, pp 95–112.

S.Lilley, *Men, Machines and History*, London, Cobbett Press, 1948.

London County Council, 'Report on the Apprentice Question', Minutes of

Proceedings of the Education Committee of the London County Council, January to June 1909, pp 412–25.

——, *Report of the Section of the Education Committee Appointed to Consider the Question of Apprenticeships* (No 925), 1909.

Alfred Marshall, *Industry and Trade*, 4th ed., London, Macmillan, 1923.

——, *Memorandum on the Fiscal Policy of International Trade*, Parliamentary Papers, 1908, Vol. CVII (321).

——, *Principles of Economics*, 8th ed., London, Macmillan, 1938.

H. J. Marshall, 'Gauges and Standards as Affecting Shop and Manufacturing Administration', *The Engineer*, 19 June 1903.

B. R. Mitchell, *Abstract of British Historical Statistics*, Cambridge, Cambridge University Press, 1962.

Mosely Industrial Commission to the United States of America, 1902, *Reports of the Delegates*, Manchester, 1903.

W. Mosses, *A History of the United Pattern Makers' Association 1872–1922*, London, 1922.

A. E. Musson, 'The Great Depression in Britain, 1873–1896: A Reappraisal', *Journal of Economic History*, Vol. 19, June 1959, pp 199–228.

The Neglect of Science, Report of Proceedings of a Conference Held . . . [at] Burlington House, 3rd May 1916, London, Harrison, 1916.

H. F. L. Orcutt, 'Modern Machine Methods', *The Engineer*, 24 January 1902, p 92; 31 January 1902, pp 122–4; 7 February 1902, pp 132–4.

D. Pollock, *The Shipbuilding Industry. Its History, Practice, Science and Finance*, London, Methuen, 1905.

E. A. Pratt, *Trade Unionism and British Industry*, London, Murray, 1904.

Report of the Tariff Commission, London, King.

    Vol. 1, *Iron and Steel Trades* (1904).

    Vol. 2, *The Textile Trades* (1905).

    Vol. 4, *The Engineering Industries* (1909).

    Vol. 6, *The Glass Industry* (1907).

L. Rostas, *Comparative Productivity in British and American Industry*, Cambridge, Cambridge University Press, 1948.

W. W. Rostow, *British Economy in the Nineteenth Century*, Oxford, Oxford University Press, 1948.

E. Rothbarth, 'Causes of the Superior Efficiency of USA Industry as Compared with British Industry', *Economic Journal*, Vol. 56, September 1946, pp 383–90.

J. Rowan, 'The Premium Plan at the Works of David Rowan & Co., Glasgow, Scotland', in J. R. Commons, *op. cit.*, pp 285–8.

——, 'Premium System Applied to Engineering Workshops', *The Engineer*, 27 March 1903, pp 325–6.

J. W. F. Rowe, *Wages in Practice and Theory*, London, Routledge, 1928.

Royal Commission on the Depression of Trade and Industry, *Second Report, Minutes of Evidence and Appendix, Part I* [Cd. 4715] 1886.

Royal Commission on Labour.

Minutes of Evidence Taken Before Group 'A' (Mining, Iron, Engineering, Hardware, Shipbuilding, and Cognate Trades), Vol. II [Cd. 6795–iv] 1892; Vol. III [Cd. 6894–vii] 1893.

Minutes of Evidence Taken Before Group 'C' (Textile, Clothing, Building, and Miscellaneous Trades), Vol. I [Cd. 6708–vi] 1892; Vol. II [Cd. 6795–vi] 1893; Vol. III [Cd. 6894–ix] 1893.

Answers to Schedules of Questions, Group 'A' [Cd. 6795–vii] 1892.

Answers to Schedules of Questions, Group 'C' [Cd. 6795–ix] 1892.

Royal Commission on the Poor Laws and Relief of Distress.

Appendix Vol. VIII, *Minutes of Evidence* [Cd. 5066] 1910.

Appendix Vol. IX, *Minutes of Evidence* [Cd. 5068] 1910.

Appendix Vol. XX, *Report by Mr Cyril Jackson on Boy Labour* [Cd. 4632] 1909.

Royal Commission on Trade Disputes and Trade Combinations, *Minutes of Evidence together with Index and Appendices* [Cd. 2826] 1906; *Report* [Cd. 2825] 1906.

W. E. G. Salter, *Productivity and Technical Change*, Cambridge, Cambridge University Press, 1960.

S. B. Saul, 'The American Impact on British Industry 1895–1914', *Business History*, Vol. 3, December 1960, pp 19–38.

J. Saville, 'Some Retarding Factors in the British Economy Before 1914', *Yorkshire Bulletin of Economic and Social Research*, Vol. 13, May 1961, pp 51–9.

D. F. Schloss, *Methods of Industrial Remuneration*, 3rd ed., London, Williams and Northgate, 1898.

'Scientific Management', *The New Statesman*, 17 June 1916.

A. Shadwell, 'History of Industrialism', in *An Encyclopaedia of Industrialism* (London, Nelson, 1913), pp 288–309.

——, *Industrial Efficiency. A Comparative Study of Industrial Life in England, Germany, and America*, new ed., London, Longmans, 1909.

——, 'The Welfare of Factory Workers', *Edinburgh Review*, October 1916, pp 361–81.

C. Singer, E. J. Holmyard, A. R. Hall, and T. I. Williams (eds.), *A History of Technology*, Vol. 5, *The Late Nineteenth Century c. 1850 to c. 1900*, Oxford, Clarendon, 1958.

R. M. Solow, 'Technical Change and the Aggregate Production Function', *Review of Economics and Statistics*, Vol. 39, August 1957, pp 312–20.

——, 'Investment and Technical Progress', in K. J. Arrow, S. Karlin, and P. Suppes, *Mathematical Methods in the Social Sciences, 1959* (Stanford, Stanford University Press, 1960), pp 89–104.

M.L. Stecker, 'The Founders, the Molders, and the Molding Machine', in J.R. Commons, *op. cit.*, second series, 1921, pp 278–308.

J. Steindl, *Small Business and Big. Economic Problems of the Size of Firms*, New York, Oxford University Press, 1945.

I. Svennilson, *Growth and Stagnation in the European Economy*, Geneva, United Nations Economic Commission for Europe, 1954.

F.W. Taussig, 'Labour Costs in the United States Compared with Costs Elsewhere', *Quarterly Journal of Economics*, Vol. 39, November 1924, pp 96–114.

R.H. Tawney, 'The Economics of Boy Labour', *Economic Journal*, Vol. 19, 1909, pp 517–37.

F.W. Taylor, *The Principles of Scientific Management*, New York, Harper, 1913.

——, *Shop Management*, New York, Harper, 1911.

G.W. Terborgh, 'Capitalism and Innovation', *American Economic Review*, Vol. 40, May 1950, pp 118–23.

Brinley Thomas, *Migration and Economic Growth*, Cambridge, Cambridge University Press, 1954.

C.B. Thompson, *The Theory and Practice of Scientific Management*, Cambridge, Houghton Mifflin, 1917.

H.J. Thompson, 'Jigs and Fixtures', *Proceedings of the Institution of Mechanical Engineers*, December 1914, pp 983–96.

Trades Union Congress, *Proceedings* (annual).

Trades Union Congress, Joint Committee on the Premium Bonus System, *Report of the Investigations and Findings of the Committee Appointed at a Meeting of the Trades Concerned*, Manchester, 1910.

F.J. Turner, *The Frontier in American History*, New York, Holt, 1920.

UK, Annual Reports of the Chief Inspector of Factories and Workshops.

——, *Census of Production, 1907*, Final Report with Tables [Cd. 6320] 1912–3.

——, Board of Trade, *Report of the Departmental Committee Appointed by the Board of Trade to Consider the Position of the Coal Trade After the War* [Cd. 9093] 1918.

——, *Report of the Departmental Committee Appointed by the Board of Trade to Consider the Position of the Electrical Trades After the War* [Cd. 9072] 1918.

——, *Report of the Departmental Committee Appointed by the Board of Trade to Consider the Position of the Engineering Trades After the War* [Cd. 9073] 1918.

——, *Report of the Departmental Committee Appointed by the Board of Trade to Consider the Position of the Iron and Steel Trades After the War* [Cd. 9071] 1918.

——, *Report of the Departmental Committee Appointed by the Board of*

Trade to Consider the Position of the Shipping and Shipbuilding Industries After the War [Cd. 9072] 1918.

UK, Board of Trade (Labour Dept.), *Report on Collective Agreements Between Employers and Workpeople in the United Kingdom* [Cd. 5366] 1910.

——, *Report of an Enquiry by the Board of Trade into the Earnings and Hours of Labour of Workpeople of the United Kingdom, 1906*. VI. *Metal, Engineering and Shipbuilding Trades in 1906* [Cd. 5814] 1914.

——, *Report on Standard Piece Rates of Wages and Sliding Scales in the United Kingdom (1900)* [Cd. 144] 1900.

——, Annual Reports of Proceedings under the Conciliation (Trade Disputes) Act, 1896.

——, Annual Reports on Strikes and Lock-outs in the United Kingdom, and on Conciliation and Arbitration Boards.

——, Ministry of Reconstruction, *Scientific Business Management (Reconstruction Problems*, No 28), London, HMSO, 1919.

United Nations, Dept. of Social Affairs, Population Division, *The Determinants and Consequences of Population Trends* (Population Studies, No 17), New York, United Nations, 1953.

US Bureau of the Census, *Census of Manufacturers*, 1905, Part I, *United States by Industries*, Washington, DC, Government Printing Office, 1907.

——, *Historical Statistics of the United States, Colonial Times to 1957*, Washington, DC, Government Printing Office, 1960.

L. Urwick and E. F. L. Brech, *The Making of Scientific Management*, Vol. 1, *Thirteen Pioneers*; Vol. 2, *Management in British Industry*; London, Management Publications Trust, 1945–8.

T. Veblen, *Imperial Germany and the Industrial Revolution*, New York, Viking, 1942.

P. V. Vernon, 'Automatic Lathe Work', *The Engineer*, November 1910, pp 553–4.

W. F. Watson, *The Worker and Wage Incentives*, London, Woolf, 1934.

S. and B. Webb, *The History of Trade Unionism*, London, Longmans, 1920.

——, *Industrial Democracy*, new ed., London, Longmans, 1919.

Sidney Webb, *The Works Manager To-day*, London, Longmans, 1918.

J. H. Wicksteed, 'Double-Cutting and High-Speed Planing Machines', *The Engineer*, 24 November 1911, pp 546–7; 22 December 1911, pp 643–4.

A. Williams, *Life in a Railway Factory*, London, Duckworth, 1915.

B. Wootton, *The Social Foundations of Wages Policy*, London, Allen & Unwin, 1955.

A. A. Young, 'Increasing Returns and Economic Progress', *Economic Journal*, Vol. 38, December 1928, pp 527–42.

Acknowledgements

The author gratefully acknowledges the permission he has received from the following to make use of published material (principally statistical data):

Professor E. H. Phelps Brown and the editors of the *Oxford Economic Papers* and the *Economic Journal* (E. H. Phelps Brown with S. J. Handfield-Jones, 'The Climacteric of the 1890's: A Study in the Expanding Economy', *Oxford Economic Papers*, n.s., Oct. 1952; E. H. Phelps Brown and B. Weber, 'Accumulation, Productivity and Distribution in the British Economy', *Economic Journal*, June 1953); Harvard University Press (A. W. Flux, 'Industrial Productivity in Great Britain and the United States', *Quarterly Journal of Economics*, Nov. 1939); Cambridge University Press (L. Rostas, *Comparative Productivity in British and American Industry*, National Institute of Economic and Social Research, *Occasional Papers* XIII, 1948; and A. K. Cairncross, *Home and Foreign Investment, 1870-1913*, 1953); Princeton University Press (R. W. Goldsmith, D. S. Brady and H. Mendershausen, *A Study of Saving in the United States*, vol. 3, 1956; S. Kuznets, 'International Differences in Capital Formation and Financing'; and R. W. Goldsmith, 'Financial Structure and Economic Growth in Advanced Countries. An Experiment in Comparative Financial Morphology', in *Capital Formation and Economic Growth. A Conference of the Universities—National Bureau Committee for Economic Research*, 1955); The United Nations Economic Commission for Europe (I. Svennilson, *Growth and Stagnation in the European Economy*, 1954); Professor Marvin Frankel (*British and American Manufacturing Productivity. A Comparison and Interpretation*, Bureau of Economic and Business Research, University of Illinois, Urbana, Illinois, 1957).

Index

LEVINE, T,

Al.

300118628T